OTHER SUN BOOKS TITLES
which you may find of interest:

THE MESSAGE OF AQUARIA by H.A. & F.H. Curtiss
Chapters on The Mystic Life, The Sign Aquarius, Are These the Last Days?, The Birth of the New Age, Masters of Wisdom, The Spiral of Life and Life Waves, Message of the Sphinx, True Brotherhood, etc.

MANUAL OF ASTROLOGY by Sepharial
Language of the Heavens, Divisions of the Zodiac, Planets, Houses, Aspects, Calculation & Reading of the Horoscope, Law of Sex, etc.

BROTHERHOOD OF MT. SHASTA by Eugene E. Thomas
Finding the Brotherhood, The Lake of Gold, The Initiation, Memories of the Past, In Advance of the Future, The Lost Lemuria, etc.

ROLLING THUNDER: THE COMING EARTH CHANGES
by J. R. Jochmans The Coming Famine and Earth Movements, The Destruction of California and New York, Future War, Nostradamus, Bible, Edgar Cayce, Coming Avatars, Pyramid Prophecy, Weather, Coming False Religion and the Antichrist, and much, much more!

THE LIGHT OF EGYPT (2 Vol. Set) **by Thomas H. Burgoyne**
Realms of Spirit and Matter, The Mysteries of Sex, Incarnation and Re-Incarnation, Karma, Influence of Stars, Symbolism and Alchemy, The Planetary Rulers, The Secret of the Soul, Mediumship, etc.

MAN, MINERALS, AND MASTERS by Charles W. Littlefield, M.D.
School of the Magi, Three Masters, The Cubes, Initiation in Tibet, Hindustan, and Egypt, History Prophecy, Numerology, Perfection.

ETIDORHPA OR THE END OF EARTH by John Uri Lloyd
Journey toward the center of the Earth thru mighty mushroom forests with an entire series of fantastic experiences. A true classic!

CONCENTRATION AND MEDITATION by Christmas Humphries
Right Motive, Power of Thought, Dangers and Safeguards, Exercises, Posture, Breathing, Color, Stillness, Taoism, Mysticism, etc.

THE ILLUMINOIDS — SECRET SOCIEITIES AND POLITICAL PARANOIA by Neal Wilgus Detailed picture of Weishaupt's Order of the Illuminati as well as other secret societies thruout history. "The best single reference on the Illuminati"--Robert Anton Wilson.

FROM POVERTY TO POWER by James Allen (Author of "As a Man Thinketh") Chapters on Silent Power of Thought, Controlling and Directing One's Forces, Secret of Health, Success, and Happiness.

PSYCHIC GROWTH by Kenneth Naysmith
Spirit of Mother Earth, Immortal Flame: Sex and Yoga, Some Psychic Dangers, Marriage, Duality, and Humility, Fall of a Titan, etc.

For a **FREE LIST** of other Sun Books titles write: **Book List, SUN PUBLISHING CO., P.O. Box 4383, Albuquerque, N.M. 87196**

MEDITATION FOR HEALING by Justin F. Stone
Contains What is Meditation, Different Modes of Meditation, Circulating the Chi, Working with the Breath, Mantra and Breath Counting, Fixation, Visualization, Chanting, Mind Control, Zen Instruction, Moving Meditation, etc.

THE KEY TO THE UNIVERSE by H.A. & F.H. Curtiss
Origin of Numerical Systems, Symbol of the "O", Letters of the Tarot, Numbers 1 thru 10, The 7 Principles of Man, The 7 Rishis, etc

THE KEY OF DESTINY by H.A. & F.H. Curtiss
The Initiate, Twelve-fold Division of the Zodiac, Reincarnation and Transmutation, The Solar System, The Letters of the Tarot, Numbers 11 thru 22, Twelve Tribes, Temperance, Man the Creator, etc.

COSMIC SYMBOLISM by Sepharial
Meaning and Purpose of Occultism, Cosmic Symbology, The Law of Cycles, Kabalism, Involution and Evolution, Planetary Numbers, Law of Vibrations, Astrology and the Law of Sex, Environment, etc.

PRINCIPLES OF OCCULT HEALING by Mary Weeks Burnett, M.D.
Occult Healing and Occultism, The Indesturctible Self, Auras and the Ethers, Healing by Prayer, Thought Forms & Color Healing, etc.

WHAT IS OCCULTISM? by Papus
Definition, Philosophy, Ethics, Aesthetics, Theodicy, Sociology, Practice of Occultism, The Traditions of Magic, Occult Viewpoint.

THE BUDDHA'S GOLDEN PATH by Dwight Goddard
Siddhatha Gautama, Right Ideas, Speech, Behavior, Vocation, Conduct, Mindfulness, Concentration, Environment, Behavior, etc.

THE SUCCESS PROCESS by Brown Landone
Five Factors Which Guarantee Success, Process of Vivid Thinking, Tones and Action, Overcoming Hinderences, Leadership, etc.

THE PRACTICE OF AUTOSUGGESTION BY THE METHOD OF EMILE COUE by C. Harry Brooks Coue's Clinic, Cures, Thought as a Force, The Will, General Formula, Dealing with Pain, Children, etc

FROM PASSION TO PEACE by James Allen (Author of "As a Man Thinketh") Passion, Aspiration, Temptation, Transmutation, Transcendence, Beatitude, Peace.

BYGONE BELIEFS — AN EXCURSION INTO THE OCCULT AND ALCHEMICAL NATURE OF MAN by H. Stanley Redgrove
Mediaeval Thought, Pythagoras, Medicine and Magic, Birds, Sympathy, Belief in Talismans, Ceremonial Magic, Architectural Symbolism, The Philosopher's Stone, Phallic Elements, plus many illus.

BYGONE BELIEFS

FIG. 1.

Symbolic Alchemical Design from *Mutus Liber* (1677).

BYGONE BELIEFS

BEING A SERIES OF
EXCURSIONS IN THE BYWAYS
OF THOUGHT

BY

H. STANLEY REDGROVE

B.Sc. (Lond.), F.C.S.

AUTHOR OF

"ALCHEMY: ANCIENT AND MODERN"
"A MATHEMATICAL THEORY OF SPIRIT"
"THE MAGIC OF EXPERIENCE," ETC.

WITH MANY ILLUSTRATIONS

SUN BOOKS
SUN PUBLISHING COMPANY
Albuquerque

First Sun Books Printing — April 1981

Copyright © 1981 by Sun Publishing Company

SUN BOOKS
are published by
SUN PUBLISHING CO.
P.O. Box 4383,
Albuquerque, N.M.
87196

Originally published in
London, England, in 1920

Printed in the United States of America

Alle Erfahrung ist Magie, und nur magisch erklärbar.
NOVALIS (Friedrich von Hardenberg).

Everything possible to be believ'd is an image of truth.
WILLIAM BLAKE.

PREFACE

THESE Excursions in the Byways of Thought were undertaken at different times and on different occasions; consequently, the reader may be able to detect in them inequalities of treatment. He may feel that I have lingered too long in some byways and hurried too rapidly through others, taking, as it were, but a general view of the road in the latter case, whilst examining everything that could be seen in the former with, perhaps, undue care. As a matter of fact, however, all these excursions have been undertaken with one and the same object in view, that, namely, of understanding aright and appreciating at their true worth some of the more curious byways along which human thought has travelled. It is easy for the superficial thinker to dismiss much of the thought of the past (and, indeed, of the present) as *mere* superstition, not worth the trouble of investigation: but it is not scientific. There is a reason for every belief, even the most fantastic, and it should be our object to discover this reason. How far, if at all, the reason in any case justifies us in holding a similar belief is, of course, another question. Some of the beliefs I have dealt with I have treated at greater length than others, because it seems to me that the truths of which they are the images—vague and distorted in many cases though they be—are truths which we have either forgotten nowadays, or are in danger of forgetting. We moderns may, indeed, learn something from the thought of the past, even in its most fantastic aspects. In one excursion at least, namely, the essay on " The Cambridge Platonists," I have ventured to deal with a higher phase—perhaps I should say the highest phase—of the thought of a bygone age, to which the modern world may be completely debtor.

" Some Characteristics of Mediæval Thought," and the two essays on Alchemy, have appeared in *The Journal of the Alchemical Society*. In others I have utilised material I have contributed to *The Occult Review*, to the editor of which journal my thanks are due for permission so to do. I have also to express my gratitude to the Rev. A. H. COLLINS, and others to be referred to in due course, for permission here to reproduce illustrations of which they are the copyright holders. I have further to offer my hearty thanks to Mr B. R. ROWBOTTOM and my wife for valuable assistance in reading the proofs.

H. S. R.

BLETCHLEY, BUCKS,
    December 1919.

CONTENTS

xi

TO

MY WIFE

LIST OF ILLUSTRATIONS

xiii

BYGONE BELIEFS

I

SOME CHARACTERISTICS OF MEDIÆVAL THOUGHT

IN the earliest days of his upward evolution man was satisfied with a very crude explanation of natural phenomena—that to which the name " animism " has been given. In this stage of mental development all the various forces of Nature are personified : the rushing torrent, the devastating fire, the wind rustling the forest leaves—in the mind of the animistic savage all these are personalities, spirits, like himself, but animated by motives more or less antagonistic to him.

I suppose that no possible exception could be taken to the statement that modern science renders animism impossible. But let us inquire in exactly what sense this is true. It is not true that science robs natural phenomena of their spiritual significance. The mistake is often made of supposing that science explains, or endeavours to explain, phenomena. But that is the business of philosophy. The task science attempts is the simpler one of the correlation of natural phenomena, and in this effort leaves the ultimate problems of metaphysics untouched. A universe, however, whose phenomena are not only capable of some degree of correlation, but present the extraordinary degree of harmony and unity which science makes manifest in Nature, cannot be, as in animism, the product of a vast number of inco-ordinated and antagonistic wills, but must either be the product of one Will, or not the product of will at all.

The latter alternative means that the Cosmos is inexplicable, which not only man's growing experience, but the fact that man and the universe form essentially a unity, forbid us to believe. The term " anthropomorphic " is too easily applied to philosophical systems, as if it constituted a criticism of their validity. For if it be true, as all must admit, that the unknown can only be explained in terms of the known, then the universe must either be explained in terms of man—*i.e.* in terms of will or desire—or remain incomprehensible. That is to say, a philosophy must either be anthropomorphic, or no philosophy at all.

Thus a metaphysical scrutiny of the results of modern science leads us to a belief in God. But man felt the need of unity, and crude animism, though a step in the right direction, failed to satisfy his thought, long before the days of modern science. The spirits of animism, however, were not discarded, but were modified, co-ordinated, and worked into a system as servants of the Most High. Polytheism may mark a stage in this process ; or, perhaps, it was a result of mental degeneracy.

What I may term systematised as distinguished from crude animism persisted throughout the Middle Ages. The work of systematisation had already been accomplished, to a large extent, by the Neo-Platonists and whoever were responsible for the Kabala. It is true that these main sources of magical or animistic philosophy remained hidden during the greater part of the Middle Ages; but at about their close the youthful and enthusiastic CORNELIUS AGRIPPA (1486–1535)[1] slaked his thirst thereat and produced his own attempt at the systematisation of magical belief in the famous *Three Books of Occult Philosophy*. But the waters of magical philosophy reached the mediæval mind through various devious channels, traditional on the one hand and literary on the other. And of the latter, the works of pseudo-DIONYSIUS,[2] whose immense influence upon mediæval thought has sometimes been neglected, must certainly be noted.

The most obvious example of a mediæval animistic belief is that in " elementals "—the spirits which personify the primordial forces of Nature, and are symbolised by the four elements, immanent in which they were supposed to exist, and through which they were held to manifest their powers. And astrology, it must be remembered, is essentially a systematised

[1] The story of his life has been admirably told by HENRY MORLEY (2 vols., 1856).

[2] These writings were first heard of in the early part of the sixth century, and were probably the work of a Syrian monk of that date, who fathered them on to DIONYSIUS the Areopagite as a pious fraud. See Dean INGE'S *Christian Mysticism* (1899), pp. 104–122, and VAUGHAN'S *Hours with the Mystics* (7th ed., 1895), vol. i. pp. 111–124. The books have been translated into English by the Rev. JOHN PARKER (2 vols., 1897–1899), who believes in the genuineness of their alleged authorship.

animism. The stars, to the ancients, were not
material bodies like the earth, but spiritual beings.
PLATO (427–347 B.C.) speaks of them as " gods ".
Mediæval thought did not regard them in quite this
way. But for those who believed in astrology, and
few, I think, did not, the stars were still symbols of
spiritual forces operative on man. Evidences of the
wide extent of astrological belief in those days are
abundant, many instances of which we shall doubt-
less encounter in our excursions.

It has been said that the theological and philosophical atmosphere of the Middle Ages was " scholastic," not mystical. No doubt " mysticism," as a
mode of life aiming at the realisation of the presence
of God, is as distinct from scholasticism as empiri-
cism is from rationalism, or " tough-minded " philosophy (to use JAMES' happy phrase) is from " tender-
minded ". But no philosophy can be absolutely and
purely deductive. It must start from certain empiri-
cally determined facts. A man might be an extreme
empiricist in religion (*i.e.* a mystic), and yet might
attempt to deduce all other forms of knowledge from
the results of his religious experiences, never caring
to gather experience in any other realm. Hence the
breach between mysticism and scholasticism is not
really so wide as may appear at first sight. Indeed,
scholasticism officially recognised three branches of
theology, of which the *mystical* was one. I think
that mysticism and scholasticism both had a profound influence on the mediæval mind, sometimes
acting as opposing forces, sometimes operating harmoniously with one another. As Professor WINDEL-
BAND puts it : " We no longer onesidedly characterise

F IG. 2.

Frontispiece to G LANVIL'S *Saducismus Triumphatus* (3rd edition, 1700),
illustrating Superstitions concerning Witchcraft, *etc.*

the philosophy of the middle ages as scholasticism, but rather place mysticism beside it as of equal rank, and even as being the more fruitful and promising movement." [1]

Alchemy, with its four Aristotelian or scholastic elements and its three mystical principles—sulphur, mercury, salt,—must be cited as the outstanding product of the combined influence of mysticism and scholasticism: of mysticism, which postulated the unity of the Cosmos, and hence taught that everything natural is the expressive image and type of some supernatural reality; of scholasticism, which taught men to rely upon deduction and to restrict experimentation to the smallest possible limits.

The mind naturally proceeds from the known, or from what is supposed to be known, to the unknown. Indeed, as I have already indicated, it must so proceed if truth is to be gained. Now what did the men of the Middle Ages regard as falling into the category of the known? Why, surely, the truths of revealed religion, whether accepted upon authority or upon the evidence of their own experience. The realm of spiritual and moral reality: there, they felt, they were on firm ground. Nature was a realm unknown; but they had analogy to guide, or, rather, misguide them. Nevertheless if, as we know, it misguided, this was not, I think, because the mystical doctrine of the correspondence between the spiritual and the natural is unsound, but because these ancient seekers into Nature's secrets knew so little, and so frequently misapplied what they did know. So alchemical

[1] Professor WILHELM WINDELBAND, Ph.D.: "Present-Day Mysticism," *The Quest*, vol. iv. (1913), p. 205.

philosophy arose and became systematised, with its wonderful endeavour to perfect the base metals by the Philosopher's Stone—the concentrated Essence of Nature,—as man's soul is perfected through the life-giving power of JESUS CHRIST.

I want, in conclusion to these brief introductory remarks, to say a few words concerning phallicism in connection with my topic. For some " tender-minded " [1] and, to my thought, obscure, reason the subject is tabooed. Even the British Museum does not include works on phallicism in its catalogue, and special permission has to be obtained to consult them. Yet the subject is of vast importance as concerns the origin and development of religion and philosophy, and the extent of phallic worship may be gathered from the widespread occurrence of obelisks and similar objects amongst ancient relics. Our own maypole dances may be instanced as one survival of the ancient worship of the male generative principle.

What could be more easy to understand than that, when man first questioned as to the creation of the earth, he should suppose it to have been generated by some process analogous to that which he saw held in the case of man ? How else could he account for its origin, if knowledge must proceed from the known to the unknown ? No one questions at all that the worship of the human generative organs as symbols of the dual generative principle of Nature degenerated into orgies of the most frightful character, but the view of Nature which thus degenerated

[1] I here use the term with the extended meaning Mr H. G. WELLS has given to it. See *The New Machiavelli.*

is not, I think, an altogether unsound one, and very interesting remnants of it are to be found in mediæval philosophy.

These remnants are very marked in alchemy. The metals, as I have suggested, are there regarded as types of man ; hence they are produced from seed, through the combination of male and female principles—mercury and sulphur, which on the spiritual plane are intelligence and love. The same is true of that Stone which is perfect Man. As BERNARD of TRÉVISAN (1406–1490) wrote in the fifteenth century : " This Stone then is compounded of a Body and Spirit, or of a volatile and fixed Substance, and that is therefore done, because nothing in the World can be generated and brought to light without these two Substances, to wit, a Male and Female : From whence it appeareth, that although these two Substances are not of one and the same species, yet one Stone doth thence arise, and although they appear and are said to be two Substances, yet in truth it is but one, to wit, *Argent-vive*."[1] No doubt this sounds fantastic ; but with all their seeming intellectual follies these old thinkers were no fools. The fact of sex is the most fundamental fact of the universe, and is a spiritual and physical as well as a physiological fact. I shall deal with the subject as concerns the speculations of the alchemists in some detail in a later excursion.

---

[1] BERNARD, Earl of TRÉVISAN: *A Treatise of the Philosopher's Stone*, 1683. (See *Collectanea Chymica : A Collection of Ten Several Treatises in Chemistry*, 1684, p. 91.)

II

PYTHAGORAS AND HIS PHILOSOPHY

IT is a matter for enduring regret that so little is known to us concerning PYTHAGORAS. What little we do know serves but to enhance for us the interest of the man and his philosophy, to make him, in many ways, the most attractive of Greek thinkers ; and, basing our estimate on the extent of his influence on the thought of succeeding ages, we recognise in him one of the world's master-minds.

PYTHAGORAS was born about 582 B.C. at Samos, one of the Grecian isles. In his youth he came in contact with THALES—the Father of Geometry, as he is well called,—and though he did not become a member of THALES' school, his contact with the latter no doubt helped to turn his mind towards the study of geometry. This interest found the right ground for its development in Egypt, which he visited when still young. Egypt is generally regarded as the birthplace of geometry, the subject having, it is supposed, been forced on the minds of the Egyptians by the necessity of fixing the boundaries of lands against the annual overflowing of the Nile. But the Egyptians were what is called an essentially practical people, and their geometrical knowledge did not extend beyond a few empirical rules useful for fixing these boundaries and in constructing their temples. Striking evidence of this fact is supplied by the AHMES papyrus, compiled some little time before 1700 B.C. from an older work dating from about 3400 B.C.,[1] a papyrus which almost certainly represents the highest mathematical knowledge reached by the Egyptians of that day. Geometry is treated very superficially and as of subsidiary interest to arithmetic ; there is no ordered series of reasoned geometrical propositions given—nothing, indeed, beyond isolated rules, and of these some are wanting in accuracy.

One geometrical fact known to the Egyptians was that if a triangle be constructed having its sides 3, 4, and 5 units long respectively, then the angle opposite the longest side is exactly a right angle ; and the Egyptian builders used this rule for constructing walls perpendicular to each other, employing a cord graduated in the required manner. The Greek mind was not, however, satisfied with the bald statement of mere facts—it cared little for practical applications, but sought above all for the underlying *reason* of everything. Nowadays we are beginning to realise that the results achieved by this type of mind, the general laws of Nature's behaviour formulated by its endeavours, are frequently of immense practical importance—of far more importance than the mere rules-of-thumb beyond which so-called

---

[1] See AUGUST EISENLOHR : *Ein mathematisches Handbuch der alten Aegypter* (1877) ; J. GOW : *A Short History of Greek Mathematics* (1884) ; and V. E. JOHNSON : *Egyptian Science from the Monuments and Ancient Books* (1891).

practical minds never advance. The classic example
of the utility of seemingly useless knowledge is
afforded by Sir WILLIAM HAMILTON's discovery, or,
rather, invention of Quarternions, but no better
example of the utilitarian triumph of the theoretical
over the so-called practical mind can be adduced
than that afforded by PYTHAGORAS. Given this rule
for constructing a right angle, about whose reason
the Egyptian who used it never bothered himself,
and the mind of PYTHAGORAS, searching for its full
significance, made that gigantic geometrical discovery
which is to this day known as the Theorem of
PYTHAGORAS—the law that in every right-angled
triangle the square on the side opposite the right
angle is equal in area to the sum of the squares on the
other two sides.[1] The importance of this discovery
can hardly be overestimated. It is of fundamental
importance in most branches of geometry, and the
basis of the whole of trigonometry—the special branch
of geometry that deals with the practical mensuration
of triangles. EUCLID devoted the whole of the first
book of his *Elements of Geometry* to establishing the
truth of this theorem ; how PYTHAGORAS demon-
strated it we unfortunately do not know.

[1] Fig. 3 affords an interesting practical demonstration of
the truth of this theorem. If the reader will copy this figure,
cut out the squares on the two shorter sides of the triangle
and divide them along the lines AD, BE, EF, he will find that
the five pieces so obtained can be made exactly to fit the square
on the longest side as shown by the dotted lines. The size and
shape of the triangle ABC, so long as it has a right angle at C,
is immaterial. The lines AD, BE are obtained by continuing
the sides of the square on the side AB, *i.e.* the side opposite
the right angle, and EF is drawn at right angles to BE.

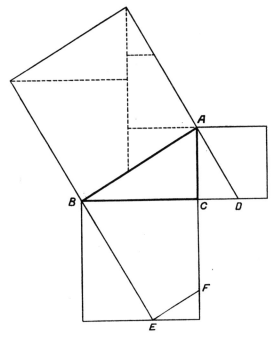

FIG. 3.
Diagram to illustrate the Theorem of PYTHAGORAS.

After absorbing what knowledge was to be gained in Egypt, PYTHAGORAS journeyed to Babylon, where he probably came into contact with even greater traditions and more potent influences and sources of knowledge than in Egypt, for there is reason for believing that the ancient Chaldeans were the builders of the Pyramids and in many ways the intellectual superiors of the Egyptians.

At last, after having travelled still further East, probably as far as India, PYTHAGORAS returned to his birthplace to teach the men of his native land the knowledge he had gained. But CRŒSUS was tyrant over Samos, and so oppressive was his rule that none had leisure in which to learn. Not a student came to PYTHAGORAS, until, in despair, so the story runs, he offered to pay an artisan if he would but learn geometry. The man accepted, and later, when PYTHAGORAS pretended inability any longer to continue the payments, he offered, so fascinating did he find the subject, to pay his teacher instead if the lessons might only be continued. PYTHAGORAS no doubt was much gratified at this ; and the motto he adopted for his great Brotherhood, of which we shall make the acquaintance in a moment, was in all likelihood based on this event. It ran, " Honour a figure and a step before a figure and a tribolus " ; or, as a freer translation renders it :—

> " A figure and a step onward :
> Not a figure and a florin."

" At all events," as Mr FRANKLAND remarks, " the motto is a lasting witness to a very singular devotion to knowledge for its own sake." [1]

[1] W. B. FRANKLAND, M.A. : *The Story of Euclid* (1902), p. 33.

But PYTHAGORAS needed a greater audience than one man, however enthusiastic a pupil he might be, and he left Samos for Southern Italy, the rich inhabitants of whose cities had both the leisure and inclination to study. Delphi, far-famed for its Oracles, was visited *en route*, and PYTHAGORAS, after a sojourn at Tarentum, settled at Croton, where he gathered about him a great band of pupils, mainly young people of the aristocratic class. By consent of the Senate of Croton, he formed out of these a great philosophical brotherhood, whose members lived apart from the ordinary people, forming, as it were, a separate community. They were bound to PYTHAGORAS by the closest ties of admiration and reverence, and, for years after his death, discoveries made by Pythagoreans were invariably attributed to the Master, a fact which makes it very difficult exactly to gauge the extent of PYTHAGORAS' own knowledge and achievements. The regime of the Brotherhood, or Pythagorean Order, was a strict one, entailing " high thinking and low living " at all times. A restricted diet, the exact nature of which is in dispute, was observed by all members, and long periods of silence, as conducive to deep thinking, were imposed on novices. Women were admitted to the Order, and PYTHAGORAS' asceticism did not prohibit romance, for we read that one of his fair pupils won her way to his heart, and, declaring her affection for him, found it reciprocated and became his wife.

SCHURÉ writes : " By his marriage with Theano, Pythagoras affixed *the seal of realization* to his work. The union and fusion of the two lives was complete. One day when the master's wife was asked what length of time elapsed before a woman could become pure after intercourse with a man, she replied : ' If it is with her husband, she is pure all the time ; if with another man, she is never pure.' "   " Many women," adds the writer, " would smilingly remark that to give such a reply one must be the wife of Pythagoras, and love him as Theano did.   And they would be in the right, for it is not marriage that sanctifies love, it is love which justifies marriage." [1]

PYTHAGORAS was not merely a mathematician : he was first and foremost a philosopher, whose philosophy found in number the basis of all things, because number, for him, alone possessed stability of relationship.   As I have remarked on a former occasion, " The theory that the Cosmos has its origin and explanation in Number . . . is one for which it is not difficult to account if we take into consideration the nature of the times in which it was formulated.   The Greek of the period, looking upon Nature, beheld no picture of harmony, uniformity and fundamental unity.   The outer world appeared to him rather as a discordant chaos, the mere sport and plaything of the gods.   The theory of the uniformity of Nature—that Nature is ever like to herself—the very essence of the modern scientific spirit, had yet to be born of years of unwearied labour and unceasing delving into Nature's innermost secrets.   Only in Mathematics—in the properties of geometrical figures, and of numbers—was the reign of law, the principle of harmony, perceivable.   Even at this present day when the marvellous has become com-

---

[1] EDOUARD SCHURÉ : *Pythagoras and the Delphic Mysteries,* trans. by F. ROTHWELL, B.A. (1906), pp. 164 and 165.

monplace, that property of right-angled triangles . . . already discussed . . . comes to the mind as a remarkable and notable fact : it must have seemed a stupendous marvel to its discoverer, to whom, it appears, the regular alternation of the odd and even numbers, a fact so obvious to us that we are inclined to attach no importance to it, seemed, itself, to be something wonderful. Here in Geometry and Arithmetic, here was order and harmony unsurpassed and unsurpassable. What wonder then that Pythagoras concluded that the solution of the mighty riddle of the Universe was contained in the mysteries of Geometry ? What wonder that he read mystic meanings into the laws of Arithmetic, and believed Number to be the explanation and origin of all that is ? " [1]

No doubt the Pythagorean theory suffers from a defect similar to that of the Kabalistic doctrine, which, starting from the fact that all words are composed of letters, representing the primary sounds of language, maintained that all the things represented by these words were created by God by means of the twenty-two letters of the Hebrew alphabet. But at the same time the Pythagorean theory certainly embodies a considerable element of truth. Modern science demonstrates nothing more clearly than the importance of numerical relationships. Indeed, " the history of science shows us the gradual transformation of crude facts of experience into increasingly exact generalisations by the application to them of mathematics. The enormous advances that have been made in recent years in physics and chemistry are very largely due to mathematical methods of

[1] *A Mathematical Theory of Spirit* (1912), pp. 64–65.

interpreting and co-ordinating facts experimentally revealed, whereby further experiments have been suggested, the results of which have themselves been mathematically interpreted. Both physics and chemistry, especially the former, are now highly mathematical. In the biological sciences and especially in psychology it is true that mathematical methods are, as yet, not so largely employed. But these sciences are far less highly developed, far less exact and systematic, that is to say, far less scientific, at present, than is either physics or chemistry. However, the application of statistical methods promises good results, and there are not wanting generalisations already arrived at which are expressible mathematically ; Weber's Law in psychology, and the law concerning the arrangement of the leaves about the stems of plants in biology, may be instanced as cases in point." [1]

The Pythagorean doctrine of the Cosmos, in its most reasonable form, however, is confronted with one great difficulty which it seems incapable of overcoming, namely, that of continuity. Modern science, with its atomic theories of matter and electricity, does, indeed, show us that the apparent continuity of material things is spurious, that all material things consist of discrete particles, and are hence measurable in numerical terms. But modern science is also obliged to postulate an ether behind

---

[1] Quoted from a lecture by the present writer on " The Law of Correspondences Mathematically Considered," delivered before The Theological and Philosophical Society on 26th April 1912, and published in *Morning Light,* vol. xxxv. (1912), p. 434 *et seq.*

these atoms, an ether which is wholly continuous, and hence transcends the domain of number.[1]   It is true that, in quite recent times, a certain school of thought has argued that the ether is also atomic in constitution—that all things, indeed, have a grained structure, even forces being made up of a large number of quantums or indivisible units of force. But this view has not gained general acceptance, and it seems to necessitate the postulation of an ether beyond the ether, filling the interspaces between its atoms, to obviate the difficulty of conceiving of action at a distance.

According to BERGSON, life—the reality that can only be lived, not understood—is absolutely continuous (*i.e.* not amenable to numerical treatment). It is because life is absolutely continuous that we cannot, he says, understand it ; for reason acts discontinuously, grasping only, so to speak, a cinematographic view of life, made up of an immense number of instantaneous glimpses.   All that passes between the glimpses is lost, and so the true whole, reason can never synthesise from that which it possesses.   On the other hand, one might also argue —extending, in a way, the teaching of the physical sciences of the period between the postulation of DALTON'S atomic theory and the discovery of the significance of the ether of space—that reality is essentially discontinuous, our idea that it is continuous being a mere illusion arising from the coarseness of our senses.   That might provide a complete vindi-

---

[1] *Cf.* chap. iii., " On Nature as the Embodiment of Number," of my *A Mathematical Theory of Spirit,* to which reference has already been made.

cation of the Pythagorean view ; but a better vindica-
tion, if not of that theory, at any rate of PYTHAGORAS'
philosophical attitude, is forthcoming, I think, in the
fact that modern mathematics has transcended the
shackles of number, and has enlarged her kingdom,
so as to include quantities other than numerical.
PYTHAGORAS, had he been born in these latter centuries, would surely have rejoiced in this enlarge-
ment, whereby the continuous as well as the discontinuous is brought, if not under the rule of
number, under the rule of mathematics indeed.

PYTHAGORAS' foremost achievement in mathematics I have already mentioned. Another notable
piece of work in the same department was the discovery of a method of constructing a parallelogram
having a side equal to a given line, an angle equal to
a given angle, and its area equal to that of a given
triangle. PYTHAGORAS is said to have celebrated
this discovery by the sacrifice of a whole ox. The
problem appears in the first book of EUCLID'S
Elements of Geometry as proposition 44. In fact,
many of the propositions of EUCLID'S first, second,
fourth, and sixth books were worked out by PYTHA-
GORAS and the Pythagoreans ; but, curiously enough,
they seem greatly to have neglected the geometry of
the circle.

The symmetrical solids were regarded by PYTHA-
GORAS, and by the Greek thinkers after him, as of the
greatest importance. To be perfectly symmetrical
or regular, a solid must have an equal number of
faces meeting at each of its angles, and these faces
must be equal regular polygons, *i.e.* figures whose
sides and angles are all equal. PYTHAGORAS, perhaps,

2

may be credited with the great discovery that there are only five such solids. These are as follows :—

The Tetrahedron, having four equilateral triangles as faces.

The Cube, having six squares as faces.

The Octahedron, having eight equilateral triangles as faces.

The Dodecahedron, having twelve regular pentagons (or five-sided figures) as faces.

The Icosahedron, having twenty equilateral triangles as faces.[1]

Now, the Greeks believed the world to be composed of four elements—earth, air, fire, water,—and to the Greek mind the conclusion was inevitable[2] that the shapes of the particles of the elements were those of the regular solids. Earth-particles were cubical, the cube being the regular solid possessed of greatest stability ; fire-particles were tetrahedral, the tetrahedron being the simplest and, hence, lightest solid. Water-particles were icosahedral for exactly the reverse reason, whilst air-particles, as intermediate between the two latter, were octahedral. The dodecahedron was, to these ancient mathematicians, the most mysterious of the solids : it was by far the most difficult to construct, the accurate drawing of the regular pentagon necessitating a rather

[1] If the reader will copy figs. 4 to 8 on cardboard or stiff paper, bend each along the dotted lines so as to form a solid, fastening together the free edges with gummed paper, he will be in possession of models of the five solids in question.

[2] *Cf.* PLATO : *The Timæus*, §§ xxviii–xxx.

PLATE 4.

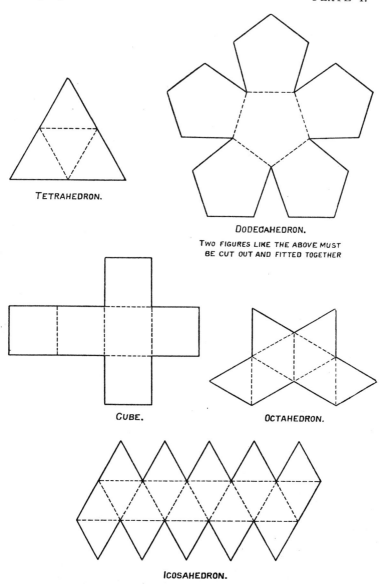

TETRAHEDRON.

DODECAHEDRON.

TWO FIGURES LIKE THE ABOVE MUST
BE CUT OUT AND FITTED TOGETHER

CUBE.

OCTAHEDRON.

ICOSAHEDRON.

FIGS. 4–8.
Diagrams for constructing the Regular (or Platonic) Solids.

elaborate application of PYTHAGORAS' great theorem.[1]
Hence the conclusion, as PLATO put it, that " this
[the regular dodecahedron] the Deity employed in
tracing the plan of the Universe." [2] Hence also
the high esteem in which the pentagon was held by
the Pythagoreans. By producing each side of this
latter figure the five-pointed star (fig. 9), known as

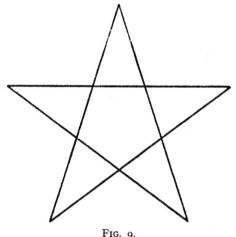

FIG. 9.
The Pentagram.

the pentagram, is obtained. This was adopted by
the Pythagoreans as the badge of their Society, and
for many ages was held as a symbol possessed of
magic powers. The mediæval magicians made use

[1] In reference to this matter FRANKLAND remarks : " In those
early days the innermost secrets of nature lay in the lap of
geometry, and the extraordinary inference follows that
Euclid's *Elements*, which are devoted to the investigation of
the regular solids, are therefore in reality and at bottom an
attempt to ' solve the universe.' Euclid, in fact, made this
goal of the Pythagoreans the aim of his *Elements*."—*Op. cit.*,
p. 35. [2] *Op. cit.*, § xxix.

of it in their evocations, and as a talisman it was held in the highest esteem.

Music played an important part in the curriculum of the Pythagorean Brotherhood, and the important discovery that the relations between the notes of musical scales can be expressed by means of numbers is a Pythagorean one. It must have seemed to its discoverer—as, in a sense, it indeed is—a striking confirmation of the numerical theory of the Cosmos. The Pythagoreans held that the positions of the heavenly bodies were governed by similar numerical relations, and that in consequence their motion was productive of celestial music. This concept of " the harmony of the spheres " is among the most celebrated of the Pythagorean doctrines, and has found ready acceptance in many mystically-speculative minds. " Look how the floor of heaven," says Lorenzo in SHAKESPEARE'S *The Merchant of Venice*—

" . . . Look how the floor of heaven
Is thick inlaid with patines of bright gold :
There's not the smallest orb which thou behold'st
But in his motion like an angel sings,
Still quiring to the young-eyed cherubins ;
Such harmony is in immortal souls ;
But whilst this muddy vesture of decay
Doth grossly close it in, we cannot hear it." [1]

Or, as KINGSLEY writes in one of his letters, " When I walk the fields I am oppressed every now and then with an innate feeling that everything I see has a meaning, if I could but understand it. And this feeling of being surrounded with truths which I cannot grasp, amounts to an indescribable awe some-

[1] Act v. scene i.

times! Everything seems to be full of God's reflex, if we could but see it. Oh! how I have prayed to have the mystery unfolded, at least hereafter. To see, if but for a moment, the whole harmony of the great system! To hear once the music which the whole universe makes as it performs His bidding!"[1] In this connection may be mentioned the very significant fact that the Pythagoreans did not consider the earth, in accordance with current opinion, to be a stationary body, but believed that it and the other planets revolved about a central point, or fire, as they called it.

As concerns PYTHAGORAS' ethical teaching, judging from the so-called *Golden Verses* attributed to him, and no doubt written by one of his disciples,[2] this would appear to be in some respects similar to that of the Stoics who came later, but free from the materialism of the Stoic doctrines. Due regard for oneself is blended with regard for the gods and for other men, the atmosphere of the whole being at once rational and austere. One verse—" Thou shalt likewise know, according to Justice, that the nature of this Universe is in all things alike "[3]—is of particular interest, as showing PYTHAGORAS' belief in that principle of analogy—that " What is below is as that which is above, what is above is as that which is below "—which held so dominant a sway over the

---

[1] CHARLES KINGSLEY: *His Letters and Memories of His Life*, edited by his wife (1883), p. 28.

[2] It seems probable, though not certain, that PYTHAGORAS wrote nothing himself, but taught always by the oral method.

[3] *Cf.* the remarks of HIEROCLES on this verse in his *Commentary*.

minds of ancient and mediæval philosophers, leading them—in spite, I suggest, of its fundamental truth —into so many fantastic errors, as we shall see in future excursions. Metempsychosis was another of the Pythagorean tenets, a fact which is interesting in view of the modern revival of this doctrine. PYTHAGORAS, no doubt, derived it from the East, apparently introducing it for the first time to Western thought.

Such, in brief, were the outstanding doctrines of the Pythagorean Brotherhood. Their teachings included, as we have seen, what may justly be called scientific discoveries of the first importance, as well as doctrines which, though we may feel compelled — perhaps rightly — to regard them as fantastic now, had an immense influence on the thought of succeeding ages, especially on Greek philosophy as represented by PLATO and the Neo-Platonists, and the more speculative minds—the occult philosophers, shall I say ?—of the latter mediæval period and succeeding centuries. The Brotherhood, however, was not destined to continue its days in peace. As I have indicated, it was a philosophical, not a political, association ; but naturally PYTHAGORAS' philosophy included political doctrines. At any rate, the Brotherhood acquired a considerable share in the government of Croton, a fact which was greatly resented by the members of the democratic party, who feared the loss of their rights ; and, urged thereto, it is said, by a rejected applicant for membership of the Order, the mob made an onslaught on the Brotherhood's place of assembly and burnt it to the ground. One account has it that PYTHAGORAS himself died in the conflagration, a sacrifice to the mad fury of the mob. According to another account—and we like to believe that this is the true one—he escaped to Tarentum, from which he was banished, to find an asylum in Metapontum, where he lived his last years in peace.

The Pythagorean Order was broken up, but the bonds of brotherhood still existed between its members. " One of them who had fallen upon sickness and poverty was kindly taken in by an innkeeper. Before dying he traced a few mysterious signs [the pentagram, no doubt] on the door of the inn and said to the host: ' Do not be uneasy, one of my brothers will pay my debts.' A year afterwards, as a stranger was passing by this inn he saw the signs and said to the host: ' I am a Pythagorean ; one of my brothers died here ; tell me what I owe you on his account.' " [1]

In endeavouring to estimate the worth of PYTHA-GORAS' discoveries and teaching, Mr FRANKLAND writes, with reference to his achievements in geometry: " Even after making a considerable allowance for his pupils' share, the Master's geometrical work calls for much admiration "; and, " . . . it cannot be far wrong to suppose that it was Pythagoras' wont to insist upon proofs, and so to secure that rigour which gives to mathematics its honourable position amongst the sciences." And of his work in arithmetic, music, and astronomy, the same author writes: " . . . everywhere he appears to have inaugurated genuinely scientific methods, and to have laid the foundations of a high and liberal education "; adding, " For nearly

[1] EDOUARD SCHURÉ: *Op. cit.*, p. 174.

a score of centuries, to the very close of the Middle Ages, the four Pythagorean subjects of study—arithmetic, geometry, astronomy, music—were the staple educational course, and were bound together into a fourfold way of knowledge—the Quadrivium." [1] With these words of due praise, our present excursion may fittingly close.

[1] *Op. cit.*, pp. 35, 37, and 38.

III

MEDICINE AND MAGIC

THERE are few tasks at once so instructive and so fascinating as the tracing of the development of the human mind as manifested in the evolution of scientific and philosophical theories. And this is, perhaps, especially true when, as in the case of medicine, this evolution has followed paths so tortuous, intersected by so many fantastic byways, that one is not infrequently doubtful as to the true road. The history of medicine is at once the history of human wisdom and the history of human credulity and folly, and the romantic element (to use the expression in its popular acceptation) thus introduced, whilst making the subject more entertaining, by no means detracts from its importance considered psychologically.

To whom the honour of having first invented medicines is due is unknown, the origins of pharmacy being lost in the twilight of myth. OSIRIS and ISIS, BACCHUS, APOLLO father of the famous physician ÆSCULAPIUS, and CHIRON the Centaur, tutor of the latter, are among the many mythological personages who have been accredited with the invention of physic. It is certain that the art of compounding medicines is extraordinarily ancient. There is a papyrus in the British Museum containing medical prescriptions which was written about 1200 B.C.; and the famous EBERS papyrus, which is devoted to medical matters, is reckoned to date from about the year 1550 B.C. It is interesting to note that in the prescriptions given in this latter papyrus, as seems to have been the case throughout the history of medicine, the principle that the efficacy of a medicine is in proportion to its nastiness appears to have been the main idea. Indeed, many old medicines contained ingredients of the most disgusting nature imaginable: a mediæval remedy known as oil of puppies, made by cutting up two newly-born puppies and boiling them with one pound of live earthworms, may be cited as a comparatively pleasant example of the remedies (?) used in the days when all sorts of excreta were prescribed as medicines.[1]

Presumably the oldest theory concerning the causation of disease is that which attributes all the ills of mankind to the malignant operations of evil spirits, a theory which someone has rather fancifully suggested is not so erroneous after all, if we may be allowed to apply the term " evil spirits " to the microbes of modern bacteriology. Remnants of this theory (which does—shall I say?—conceal a transcendental truth), that is, in its original form, still survive to the present day in various superstitious customs, whose absurdity does not need emphasising:

[1] See the late Mr A. C. WOOTTON's excellent work, *Chronicles of Pharmacy* (2 vols, 1910), to which I gladly acknowledge my indebtedness.

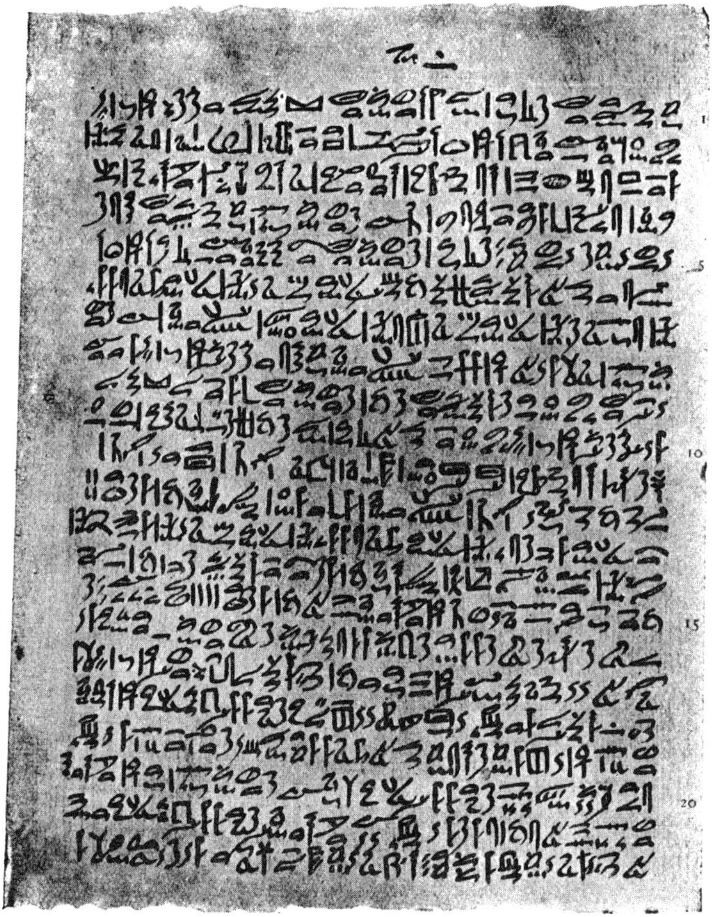

FIG. 10.
Reduced Facsimile of a Page of the Papyrus EBERS.
(By permission of Messrs Macmillan & Co.)

for example, the use of red flannel by old-fashioned
folk with which to tie up sore throats—red having
once been supposed to be a colour very angatonistic
to evil spirits ; so much so that at one time red cloth
hung in the patient's room was much employed as a
cure for smallpox !

Medicine and magic have always been closely
associated. Indeed, the greatest name in the history of pharmacy is also what is probably the greatest
name in the history of magic—the reference, of
course, being to PARACELSUS (1493–1541). Until
PARACELSUS, partly by his vigorous invective and
partly by his remarkable cures of various diseases,
demolished the old school of medicine, no one dared
contest the authority of GALEN (130–*circa* 205) and
AVICENNA (980–1037). GALEN'S theory of disease
was largely based upon that of the four humours in
man—bile, blood, phlegm, and black bile,—which
were regarded as related to (but not identical with)
the four elements—fire, air, water, and earth,—being
supposed to have characters similar to these. Thus,
to bile, as to fire, were attributed the properties of
hotness and dryness ; to blood and air those of hotness and moistness ; to phlegm and water those of
coldness and moistness ; and, finally, black bile, like
earth, was said to be cold and dry. GALEN supposed
that an alteration in the due proportion of these
humours gives rise to disease, though he did not consider this to be its only cause ; thus, cancer, it was
thought, might result from an excess of black bile,
and rheumatism from an excess of phlegm. Drugs,
GALEN argued, are of efficiency in the curing of
disease, according as they possess one or more of

these so-called fundamental properties, hotness, dryness, coldness, and moistness, whereby it was considered that an excess of any humour might be counteracted ; moreover, it was further assumed that four degrees of each property exist, and that only those drugs are of use in curing a disease which contain the necessary property or properties in the degree proportionate to that in which the opposite humour or humours are in excess in the patient's system.

PARACELSUS' views were based upon his theory (undoubtedly true in a sense) that man is a microcosm, a world in miniature.[1] Now, all things material, taught PARACELSUS, contain the three principles termed in alchemistic phraseology salt, sulphur, and mercury. This is true, therefore, of man : the healthy body, he argued, is a sort of chemical compound in which these three principles are harmoniously blended (as in the Macrocosm) in due proportion, whilst disease is due to a preponderance of one principle, fevers, for example, being the result of an excess of sulphur (*i.e.* the fiery principle), *etc*. PARACELSUS, although his theory was not so different from that of GALEN, whose views he denounced, was thus led to seek for *chemical* remedies, containing these principles in varying proportions ; he was not content with medicinal herbs and minerals in their crude state, but attempted to extract their effective essences ; indeed, he maintained that the preparation of new and better drugs is the chief business of chemistry.

This theory of disease and of the efficacy of drugs

[1] See the " Note on the Paracelsian Doctrine of the Microcosm " below.

Fig. 11.

PARACELSUS (aged 24), from a Painting by SCOREL (1517), now in the Louvre Gallery.

was complicated by many fantastic additions ; [1] thus there is the " Archæus," a sort of benevolent demon, supposed by PARACELSUS to look after all the unconscious functions of the bodily organism, who has to be taken into account. PARACELSUS also held the Doctrine of Signatures, according to which the medicinal value of plants and minerals is indicated by their external form, or by some sign impressed upon them by the operation of the stars. A very old example of this belief is to be found in the use of mandrake (whose roots resemble the human form) by the Hebrews and Greeks as a cure for sterility ; or, to give an instance which is still accredited by some, the use of eye-bright (*Euphrasia officinalis*, L., a plant with a black pupil-like spot in its corolla) for complaints of the eyes.[2] Allied to this doctrine are such beliefs, once held, as that the lungs of foxes are good for bronchial troubles, or that the heart of a lion will endow one with courage ; as CORNELIUS AGRIPPA put it, " It is well known amongst physicians that brain helps the brain, and lungs the lungs." [3]

In modern times homœopathy—according to which

[1] The question of PARACELSUS' pharmacy is further complicated by the fact that this eccentric genius coined many new words (without regard to the principles of etymology) as names for his medicines, and often used the same term to stand for quite different bodies. Some of his disciples maintained that he must not always be understood in a literal sense, in which probably there is an element of truth. See, for instance, *A Golden and Blessed Casket of Nature's Marvels*, by BENEDICTUS FIGULUS (trans. by A. E. WAITE, 1893).

[2] See Dr ALFRED C. HADDON's *Magic and Fetishism* (1906), p. 15.

[3] HENRY CORNELIUS AGRIPPA: *Occult Philosophy*, bk. i. chap. xv. (WHITEHEAD's edition, Chicago, 1898, p. 72).

a drug is a cure, if administered in small doses, for
that disease whose symptoms it produces, if given in
large doses to a healthy person—seems to bear some
resemblance to these old medical theories concerning the curing of like by like. That the system of
HAHNEMANN (1755–1843), the founder of homœopathy, is free from error could be scarcely maintained, but certain recent discoveries in connection
with serum-therapy appear to indicate that the last
word has not yet been said on the subject, and the
formula " like cures like " may still have another
lease of life to run.

To return to PARACELSUS, however. It may be
thought that his views were not so great an advance
on those of GALEN ; but whether or not this be the
case, his union of chemistry and medicine was of
immense benefit to each science, and marked a new
era in pharmacy. Even if his theories were highly
fantastic, it was he who freed medicine from the
shackles of traditionalism, and rendered progress in
medical science possible.

I must not conclude these brief notes without some
reference to the medical theory of the medicinal
efficacy of words. The EBERS papyrus already mentioned gives various formulas which must be pronounced when preparing and when administering a
drug ; and there is a draught used by the Eastern
Jews as a cure for bronchial complaints prepared by
writing certain words on a plate, washing them off
with wine, and adding three grains of a citron which
has been used at the Tabernacle festival. But enough
for our present excursion ; we must hie us back to
the modern world, with its alkaloids, serums, and

anti-toxins—another day we will, perhaps, wander again down the by-paths of Medicinal Magic.

NOTE ON THE PARACELSIAN DOCTRINE OF THE MICROCOSM

" Man's nature," writes CORNELIUS AGRIPPA, " *is the most complete Image of the whole Universe.*" [1] This theory, especially connected with the name of PARACELSUS, is worthy of more than passing reference; but as the consideration of it leads us from medicine to metaphysics, I have thought it preferable to deal with the subject in a note.

Man, taught the old mystical philosophers, is threefold in nature, consisting of spirit, soul, and body. The Paracelsian mercury, sulphur, and salt were the mineral analogues of these. " As to the Spirit," writes VALENTINE WEIGEL (1533–1588), a disciple of PARACELSUS, " we are of God, move in God, and live in God, and are nourished of God. Hence God is in us and we are in God ; God hath put and placed Himself in us, and we are put and placed in God. As to the Soul, we are from the Firmament and Stars, we live and move therein, and are nourished thereof. Hence the Firmament with its astralic virtues and operations is in us, and we in it. The Firmament is put and placed in us, and we are put and placed in the Firmament. As to the Body, we are of the elements, we move and live therein, and are nourished of them :—hence the elements are in us, and we in them. The elements, by the slime, are put and placed in us, and we are

[1] H. C. AGRIPPA: *Occult Philosophy*, bk. i. chap. xxxiii. (WHITEHEAD'S edition, p. 111).

put and placed in them." [1]   Or, to quote from PARA-
CELSUS himself, in his *Hermetic Astronomy* he writes :
" God took the body out of which He built up man
from those things which He created from nothingness
into something . . .   Hence man is now a microcosm, or a little world, because he is an extract from
all the stars and planets of the whole firmament, from
the earth and the elements, and so he is their quintessence. . . .   But between the macrocosm and the
microcosm this difference occurs, that the form,
image, species, and substance of man are diverse
therefrom.   In man the earth is flesh, the water is
blood, fire is the heat thereof, and air is the balsam.
These properties have not been changed but only
the substance of the body.   So man is man, not a
world, yet made from the world, made in the likeness,
not of the world, but of God.   Yet man comprises
in himself all the qualities of the world. . . .   His
body is from the world, and therefore must be fed
and nourished by that world from which he has
sprung. . . .   He has been taken from the earth and
from the elements, and therefore, must be nourished
by these. . . .   Now, man is not only flesh and
blood, but there is within the intellect which does not,
like the complexion, come from the elements, but
from the stars.   And the condition of the stars is
this, that all the wisdom, intelligence, industry of the
animal, and all the arts peculiar to man are contained
in them.   From the stars man has these same things,
and that is called the light of Nature ; in fact, it is

[1] VALENTINE WEIGEL : " *Astrology Theologised* " : *The
Spiritual Hermeneutics of Astrology and Holy Writ,* ed. by
ANNA BONUS KINGSFORD (1886), p. 59.

whatever man has found by the light of Nature. . . .
Such, then, is the condition of man, that, out of the
great universe he needs both elements and stars,
seeing that he himself is constituted in that way." [1]

It is not difficult to discern a certain truth in all
this, making allowances for modes of thought which
are not those of the present day. The Swedish
philosopher SWEDENBORG (1688–1772) reaffirmed the
theory in later years ; but, as he points out,[2] the
reason that man is a microcosm lies deeper than in
the facts that his body is of the elements of this earth
and is nourished thereby. According to this profound thinker, *form*, spiritually understood, is the
expression of *use*, the uses of things being indicated
by their forms. Now, the human form is the highest
of all forms, because it subserves the highest of all
uses. Hence, both the world of matter and the
world of spirit are in the human form, because there
is a correspondence in use between man and the
Cosmos. We may, therefore, call man as to his
body a microcosm, or little world ; as to his soul a
micro-uranos, or little heaven. Or we may speak
of the macrocosm, or great world, as the Grand Man,
and we may say that the Soul of this Grand Man, the
self-existent, substantial, and efficient cause of all
things, at once immanent within yet transcending all
things, is God.

[1] *The Hermetic and Alchemical Writings of* PARACELSUS, ed.
by A. E. WAITE (1894), vol. ii. pp. 289–291.

[2] See especially his *Divine Love and Wisdom*, §§ 251 and 319.

IV

SUPERSTITIONS CONCERNING BIRDS

AMONGST the most remarkable of natural occurrences must be included many of the phenomena connected with the behaviour of birds. Undoubtedly numerous species of birds are susceptible to atmospheric changes (of an electrical and barometric nature) too slight to be observed by man's unaided senses ; thus only is to be explained the phenomenon of migration and also the many other peculiarities in the behaviour of birds whereby approaching changes in the weather may be foretold. Probably, also, this fact has much to do with the extraordinary homing instinct of pigeons. But, of course, in the days when meteorological science had yet to be born, no such explanation as this could be known. The ancients observed that birds by their migrations or by other peculiarities in their behaviour prognosticated coming changes in the seasons of the year and other changes connected with the weather (such as storms, *etc.*) ; they saw, too, in the homing instincts of pigeons an apparent exhibition of intelligence exceeding that of man. What more natural, then, for them to attribute foresight to birds, and to suppose that all sorts of coming events (other than those of an atmospheric nature) might be foretold by careful observation of their flight and song?

Augury—that is, the art of divination by observing the behaviour of birds—was extensively cultivated by the Etrurians and Romans.[1] It is still used, I believe, by the natives of Samoa. The Romans had an official college of augurs, the members of which were originally three patricians. About 300 B.C. the number of patrician augurs was increased by one, and five plebeian augurs were added. Later the number was again increased to fifteen. The object of augury was not so much to foretell the future as to indicate what line of action should be followed, in any given circumstances, by the nation. The augurs were consulted on all matters of importance, and the position of augur was thus one of great consequence. In what appears to be the oldest method, the augur, arrayed in a special costume, and carrying a staff with which to mark out the visible heavens into houses, proceeded to an elevated piece of ground, where a sacrifice was made and a prayer repeated. Then, gazing towards the sky, he waited until a bird appeared. The point in the heavens where it first made its appearance was carefully noted, also the manner and direction of its flight, and the point where it was lost sight of. From these particulars an augury was derived, but, in order to be of effect, it had to be confirmed by a further one.

[1] This is not quite an accurate definition, as " auguries " were also obtained from other animals and from celestial phenomena (*e.g.* lightning), *etc.*

Auguries were also drawn from the notes of birds, birds being divided by the augurs into two classes : (i) *oscines*, " those which give omens by their note," and (ii) *alites*, " those which afford presages by their flight." [1] Another method of augury was performed by the feeding of chickens specially kept for this purpose. This was done just before sunrise by the *pullarius* or feeder, strict silence being observed. If the birds manifested no desire for their food, the omen was of a most direful nature. On the other hand, if from the greediness of the chickens the grain fell from their beaks and rebounded from the ground, the augury was most favourable. This latter augury was known as *tripudium solistimum*. " Any fraud practised by the ' pullarius '," writes the Rev. EDWARD SMEDLEY, " reverted to his own head. Of this we have a memorable instance in the great battle between Papirius Cursor and the Samnites in the year of Rome 459. So anxious were the troops for battle, that the ' pullarius ' dared to announce to the consul a ' tripudium solistimum,' although the chickens refused to eat. Papirius unhesitatingly gave the signal for fight, when his son, having discovered the false augury, hastened to communicate it to his father. ' Do thy part well,' was his reply, ' and let the deceit of the augur fall on himself. The " tripudium " has been announced to me, and no omen could be better for the Roman army and people ! ' As the troops advanced, a javelin thrown at random struck the ' pullarius ' dead. ' The hand of heaven is in the battle,' cried Papirius ; ' the guilty is punished ! '

[1] PLINY : *Natural History*, bk. x. chap. xxii. (BOSTOCK and RILEY's trans., vol. ii., 1855, p. 495).

and he advanced and conquered." [1]   A coincidence of this sort, if it really occurred, would very greatly strengthen the popular belief in auguries.

The *cock* has always been reckoned a bird possessed of magic power.   At its crowing, we are told, all unquiet spirits who roam the earth depart to their dismal abodes, and the orgies of the Witches' Sabbath terminate.   A cock is the favourite sacrifice offered to evil spirits in Ceylon and elsewhere.   Alectromancy [2] was an ancient and peculiarly senseless method of divination (so called) in which a cock was employed. The bird had to be young and quite white.   Its feet were cut off and crammed down its throat with a piece of parchment on which were written certain Hebrew words.   The cock, after the repetition of a prayer by the operator, was placed in a circle divided into parts corresponding to the letters of the alphabet, in each of which a grain of wheat was placed.   A certain psalm was recited, and then the letters were noted from which the cock picked up the grains, a fresh grain being put down for each one picked up. These letters, properly arranged, were said to give the answer to the inquiry for which divination was made.   I am not sure what one was supposed to do if, as seems likely, the cock refused to act in the required manner.

The *owl* was reckoned a bird of evil omen with the Romans, who derived this opinion from the

[1] Rev. EDWARD SMEDLEY, M.A.: *The Occult Sciences* (*Encyclopædia Metropolitana*), ed. by ELIHU RICH (1855), p. 144.
[2] *Cf.* ARTHUR EDWARD WAITE: *The Occult Sciences* (1891), pp. 124 and 125.

Etrurians, along with much else of their so-called science of augury. It was particularly dreaded if seen in a city, or, indeed, anywhere by day. PLINY (Caius Plinius Secundus, A.D. 61–before 115) informs us that on one occasion " a horned owl entered the very sanctuary of the Capitol ; . . . in consequence of which, Rome was purified on the nones of March in that year." [1]

The folk-lore of the British Isles abounds with quaint beliefs and stories concerning birds. There is a charming Welsh legend concerning the *robin,* which the Rev. T. F. T. DYER quotes from *Notes and Queries* :—" Far, far away, is a land of woe, darkness, spirits of evil, and fire. Day by day does this little bird bear in his bill a drop of water to quench the flame. So near the burning stream does he fly, that his dear little feathers are *scorched ;* and hence he is named Brou-rhuddyn (Breast-burnt). To serve little children, the robin dares approach the infernal pit. No good child will hurt the devoted benefactor of man. The robin returns from the land of fire, and therefore he feels the cold of winter far more than his brother birds. He shivers in the brumal blast ; hungry, he chirps before your door." [2]

Another legend accounts for the robin's red breast by supposing this bird to have tried to pluck a thorn from the crown encircling the brow of the crucified CHRIST, in order to alleviate His sufferings. No doubt it is on account of these legends that it is considered a

---

[1] PLINY : *Natural History,* bk. x. chap. xvi. (BOSTOCK and RILEY'S trans., vol. ii., 1855, p. 492).

[2] T. F. THISELTON DYER, M.A. : *English Folk-Lore* (1878), pp. 65 and 66.

crime, which will be punished with great misfortune, to kill a robin. In some places the same prohibition extends to the *wren*, which is popularly believed to be the wife of the robin. In other parts, however, the wren is (or at least was) cruelly hunted on certain days. In the Isle of Man the wren-hunt took place on Christmas Eve and St Stephen's Day, and is accounted for by a legend concerning an evil fairy who lured many men to destruction, but had to assume the form of a wren to escape punishment at the hands of an ingenious knight-errant.

For several centuries there was prevalent over the whole of civilised Europe a most extraordinary superstition concerning the small Arctic bird resembling, but not so large as, the common wild goose, known as the *barnacle* or *bernicle goose*. MAX MUELLER [1] has suggested that this word was really derived from *Hibernicula*, the name thus referring to Ireland, where the birds were caught ; but common opinion associated the barnacle goose with the shellfish known as the barnacle (which is found on timber exposed to the sea), supposing that the former was generated out of the latter. Thus in one old medical writer we find : " There are founde in the north parts of Scotland, and the Ilands adiacent, called Orchades [Orkney Islands], certain trees, whereon doe growe certaine shell fishes, of a white colour tending to russet ; wherein are conteined little liuing creatures : which shells in time of maturitie doe open, and out of them grow those little living things ; which falling

[1] See F. MAX MUELLER'S *Lectures on the Science of Language* (1885), where a very full account of the tradition concerning the origin of the barnacle goose will be found.

into the water, doe become foules, whom we call Barnakles . . . but the other that do fall vpon the land, perish and come to nothing : this much by the writings of others, and also from the mouths of the people of those parts. . . ." [1]

The writer, however, who was a well-known surgeon and botanist of his day, adds that he had personally examined certain shell-fish from Lancashire, and on opening the shells had observed within birds in various stages of development. No doubt he was deceived by some purely superficial resemblances—for example, the feet of the barnacle fish resemble somewhat the feathers of a bird. He gives an imaginative illustration of the barnacle fowl escaping from its shell, which is reproduced in fig. 12.

Turning now from superstitions concerning actual birds to legends of those that are purely mythical, passing reference must be made to the *roc*, a bird existing in Arabian legend, which we meet in the *Arabian Nights*, and which is chiefly remarkable for its size and strength.

The *phœnix*, perhaps, is of more interest. Of " that famous bird of Arabia," PLINY writes as follows, prefixing his description of it with the cautious remark, " I am not quite sure that its existence is not all a fable." " It is said that there is only one in existence in the whole world, and that that one has not been seen very often. We are told that this bird is of the size of an eagle, and has a brilliant golden plumage around the neck, while the rest of the body is of a purple colour ; except the tail,

[1] JOHN GERARDE: *The Herball; or, Generall Historie of Plantes* (1597), 1391.

FIG. 14.

Harpy, from VLYSSIS ALDROVANDI's *Monstrorum Historia*
(1642).

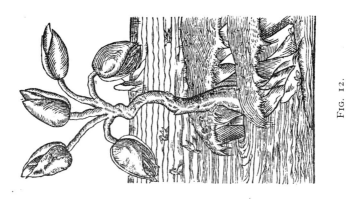

FIG. 12.

Barnacle Geese, from GERARDE's
Herball (1597).

(*By permission of the British Museum. Photographs by Donald Macbeth, London.*)

which is azure, with long feathers intermingled of a roseate hue ; the throat is adorned with a crest, and the head with a tuft of feathers. The first Roman who described this bird . . . was the senator Manilius. . . . He tells us that no person has ever seen this bird eat, that in Arabia it is looked upon as sacred to the sun, that it lives five hundred and forty years, that when it becomes old it builds a nest of cassia and sprigs of incense, which it fills with perfumes, and then lays its body down upon them to die ; that from its bones and marrow there springs at first a sort of small worm, which in time changes into a little bird ; that the first thing that it does is to perform the obsequies of its predecessor, and to carry the nest entire to the city of the Sun near Panchaia, and there deposit it upon the altar of that divinity.

" The same Manilius states also, that the revolution of the great year is completed with the life of this bird, and that then a new cycle comes round again with the same characteristics as the former one, in the seasons and the appearance of the stars. . . . This bird was brought to Rome in the censorship of the Emperor Claudius . . . and was exposed to public view. . . . This fact is attested by the public Annals, but there is no one that doubts that it was a fictitious phœnix only." [1]

The description of the plumage, *etc.*, of this bird applies fairly well, as CUVIER has pointed out,[2] to

---

[1] PLINY : *Natural History*, bk. x. chap. ii. (BOSTOCK and RILEY's trans., vol. ii., 1855, pp. 479–481).

[2] See CUVIER's *The Animal Kingdom*, GRIFFITH's trans., vol. viii. (1829), p. 23.

the golden pheasant, and a specimen of the latter may have been the " fictitious phœnix " referred to above. That this bird should have been credited with the extraordinary and wholly fabulous properties related by PLINY and others is not, however, easy to understand. The phœnix was frequently used to illustrate the doctrine of the immortality of the soul (*e.g.* in CLEMENT'S *First Epistle to the Corinthians*), and it is not impossible that originally it was nothing more than a symbol of immortality which in time became to be believed in as a really existing bird. The fact, however, that there was supposed to be only one phœnix, and also that the length of each of its lives coincided with what the ancients termed a " great year," may indicate that the phœnix was a symbol of cosmological periodicity. On the other hand, some ancient writers (*e.g.* TACITUS, A.D. 55–120) explicitly refer to the phœnix as a symbol of the sun, and in the minds of the ancients the sun was closely connected with the idea of immortality. Certainly the accounts of the gorgeous colours of the plumage of the phœnix might well be descriptions of the rising sun. It appears, moreover, that the Egyptian hieroglyphic *benu*, , which is a figure of a heron or crane (and thus akin to the phœnix), was employed to designate the rising sun.

There are some curious Jewish legends to account for the supposed immortality of the phœnix. According to one, it was the sole animal that refused to eat of the forbidden tree when tempted by EVE. According to another, its immortality was conferred on it by NOAH because of its considerate behaviour in the

Ark, the phœnix not clamouring for food like the other animals.[1]

There is a celebrated bird in Chinese tradition, the *Fung Hwang*, which some sinologues identify with the phœnix of the West.[2] According to a commentator on the *'Rh Ya*, this " felicitous and perfect bird has a cock's head, a snake's neck, a swallow's beak, a tortoise's back, is of five different colours and more than six feet high."

Another account (that in the *Lun Yü Tseh Shwai Shing*) tells us that " its head resembles heaven, its eye the sun, its back the moon, its wings the wind, its foot the ground, and its tail the woof." Furthermore, " its mouth contains commands, its heart is conformable to regulations, its ear is thoroughly acute in hearing, its tongue utters sincerity, its colour is luminous, its comb resembles uprightness, its spur is sharp and curved, its voice is sonorous, and its belly is the treasure of literature." Like the dragon, tortoise, and unicorn, it was considered to be a spiritual creature ; but, unlike the Western phœnix, more than one Fung Hwang was, as I have pointed out, believed to exist. The birds were not always to be seen, but, according to Chinese records, they made their appearance during the reigns of certain

---

[1] The existence of such fables as these shows how grossly the real meanings of the Sacred Writings have been misunderstood.

[2] Mr CHAS. GOULD, B.A., to whose book *Mythical Monsters* (1886) I am very largely indebted for my account of this bird, and from which I have culled extracts from the Chinese, is not of this opinion. Certainly the fact that we read of Fung Hwangs in the plural, whilst tradition asserts that there is only one phœnix, seems to point to a difference in origin.

sovereigns. The Fung Hwang is regarded by the
Chinese as an omen of great happiness and pro-
sperity, and its likeness is embroidered on the robes
of empresses to ensure success.   Probably, if the bird
is not to be regarded as purely mythological and
symbolic in origin, we have in the stories of it no
more than exaggerated accounts of some species of
pheasant. Japanese literature contains similar stories.

Of other fabulous bird-forms mention may be
made of the *griffin* and the *harpy*. The former was
a creature half eagle, half lion, popularly supposed to
be the progeny of the union of these two latter.   It
is described in the so-called *Voiage and Travaile of
Sir* JOHN MAUNDEVILLE in the following terms [1] :—
" Sum men seyn, that thei han the Body upward, as
an Egle, and benethe as a Lyoun : and treuly thei
seyn sothe, that thei ben of that schapp. But o
Griffoun hathe the body more gret and is more strong

---

[1] *The Voiage and Travaile of Sir* JOHN MAUNDEVILLE, *Kt.
Which treateth of the Way to Hierusalem ; and of Marvayles of
Inde, with other Ilands and Countryes. Now Publish'd entire
from an Original MS. in The Cotton Library* (London, 1727),
cap. xxvi. pp. 325 and 326.

" This work is mainly a compilation from the writings of
William of Boldensele, Friar Odoric of Pordenone, Hetoum of
Armenia, Vincent de Beauvais, and other geographers. It is
probable that the name John de Mandeville should be regarded
as a pseudonym concealing the identity of Jean de Bourgogne,
a physician at Liège, mentioned under the name of Joannes
ad Barbam in the vulgate Latin version of the Travels." (Note
in British Museum Catalogue). The work, which was first
published in French during the latter part of the fourteenth
century, achieved an immense popularity, the marvels that it
relates being readily received by the credulous folk of that and
many a succeeding day.

FIG. 13.

The Fung Hwang, according to the '*Rh Ya*, from GOULD'S
Mythical Monsters.

thanne 8 Lyouns, of suche Lyouns as ben o this half ;
and more gret and strongere, than an 100 Egles,
suche as we han amonges us.   For o Griffoun there
will bere, fleynge to his Nest, a gret Hors, or 2 Oxen
zoked to gidere, as thei gon at the Plowghe.   For he
hathe his Talouns so longe and so large and grete,
upon his Feet, as thoughe thei weren Hornes of grete
Oxen or of Bugles or of Kyzn ; so that men maken
Cuppes of hem, to drynken of : and of hire Ribbes
and of the Pennes of hire Wenges, men maken Bowes
fulle strong, to schote with Arwes and Quarelle."
The special characteristic of the griffin was its watch-
fulness, its chief function being thought to be that
of guarding secret treasure.   This characteristic, no
doubt, accounts for its frequent use in heraldry as a
supporter to the arms.   It was sacred to APOLLO,
the sun-god, whose chariot was, according to early
sculptures, drawn by griffins.   PLINY, who speaks
of it as a bird having long ears and a hooked beak,
regarded it as fabulous.

The harpies (*i.e.* snatchers) in Greek mythology are
creatures like vultures as to their bodies, but with
the faces of women, and armed with sharp claws.

" Of Monsters all, most Monstrous this ; no greater Wrath
    God sends 'mongst Men ; it comes from depth of pitchy
    Hell :
And Virgin's Face, but Womb like Gulf unsatiate hath,
    Her Hands are griping Claws, her Colour pale and fell." [1]

We meet with the harpies in the story of PHINEUS,
a son of AGENOR, King of Thrace.   At the bidding
of his jealous wife, IDÆA, daughter of DARDANUS,

[1] Quoted from VERGIL by JOHN GUILLIM in his *A Display
of Heraldry* (sixth edition, 1724), p. 271.

PHINEUS put out the sight of his children by his
former wife, CLEOPATRA, daughter of BOREAS. To
punish this cruelty, the gods caused him to become
blind, and the harpies were sent continually to harass
and affright him, and to snatch away his food or
defile it by their presence. They were afterwards
driven away by his brothers-in-law, ZETES and
CALAIS. It has been suggested that originally the
harpies were nothing more than personifications of
the swift storm-winds ; and few of the old naturalists, credulous as they were, regarded them as real
creatures, though this cannot be said of all. Some
other fabulous bird-forms are to be met with in
Greek and Arabian mythologies, *etc.*, but they are
not of any particular interest. And it is time for us
to conclude our present excursion, and to seek for
other byways.

V

THE POWDER OF SYMPATHY:
A CURIOUS MEDICAL SUPERSTITION

OUT of the superstitions of the past the science of
the present has gradually evolved. In the Middle
Ages, what by courtesy we may term medical science
was, as we have seen, little better than a heterogeneous
collection of superstitions, and although various
reforms were instituted with the passing of time,
superstition still continued for long to play a prominent part in medical practice.

One of the most curious of these old medical (or
perhaps I should say surgical) superstitions was that
relating to the Powder of Sympathy, a remedy (?)
chiefly remembered in connection with the name of
Sir KENELM DIGBY (1603–1665), though he was probably not the first to employ it. The Powder itself,
which was used as a cure for wounds, was, in fact,
nothing else than common vitriol,[1] though an im-

---

[1] Green vitriol, ferrous sulphate heptahydrate, a compound
of iron, sulphur, and oxygen, crystallised with seven molecules
of water, represented by the formula $FeSO_4 . 7H_2O$. On exposure to the air it loses water, and is gradually converted into
basic ferric sulphate. For long, green vitriol was confused
with blue vitriol, which generally occurs as an impurity in
crude green vitriol. Blue vitriol is copper sulphate penta-
hydrate, $CuSO_4 . 5H_2O$.

proved and more elegant form (if one may so describe
it) was composed of vitriol desiccated by the sun's
rays, mixed with *gum tragacanth*. It was in the
application of the Powder that the remedy was
peculiar. It was not, as one might expect, applied
to the wound itself, but any article that might have
blood from the wound upon it was either sprinkled
with the Powder or else placed in a basin of water
in which the Powder had been dissolved, and maintained at a temperate heat. Meanwhile, the wound
was kept clean and cool.

Sir KENELM DIGBY appears to have delivered a
discourse dealing with the famous Powder before a
learned assembly at Montpellier in France ; at least
a work purporting to be a translation of such a discourse was published in 1658,[1] and further editions
appeared in 1660 and 1664. KENELM was a son
of the Sir EVERARD DIGBY (1578–1606) who was
executed for his share in the Gunpowder Plot. In
spite of this fact, however, JAMES I. appears to have
regarded him with favour. He was a man of romantic temperament, possessed of charming manners,
considerable learning, and even greater credulity.
His contemporaries seem to have differed in their
opinions concerning him. EVELYN (1620–1706), the
diarist, after inspecting his chemical laboratory,
rather harshly speaks of him as " an errant mounte-
bank ". Elsewhere he well refers to him as " a teller

---

[1] *A late Discourse . . . by Sir* KENELM DIGPY, *Kt. &c.
Touching the Cure of Wounds by the Powder of Sympathy . . .
rendered . . . out of French into English by* R. WHITE, *Gent.*
(1658). This is entitled the second edition, but appears to
have been the first.

FIG. 15.

Sir KENELM DIGBY, from an engraved Portrait by HOUBRAKEN,
after VANDYKE.

of strange things "—this was on the occasion of DIGBY's relating a story of a lady who had such an aversion to roses that one laid on her cheek produced a blister !

To return to the *Late Discourse* : after some preliminary remarks, Sir KENELM records a cure which he claims to have effected by means of the Powder. It appears that JAMES HOWELL (1594–1666, afterwards historiographer royal to CHARLES II.), had, in the attempt to separate two friends engaged in a duel, received two serious wounds in the hand. To proceed in the writer's own words :—" It was my chance to be lodged hard by him ; and four or five days after, as I was making myself ready, he [Mr Howell] came to my House, and prayed me to view his wounds ; for I understand, said he, that you have extraordinary remedies upon such occasions, and my Surgeons apprehend some fear, that it may grow to a Gangrene, and so the hand must be cut off. . . .

" I asked him then for any thing that had the blood upon it, so he presently sent for his Garter, wherewith his hand was first bound : and having called for a Bason of water, as if I would wash my hands ; I took an handfull of Powder of Vitrol, which I had in my study, and presently dissolved it. As soon as the bloody garter was brought me, I put it within the Bason, observing in the interim what Mr *Howel* did, who stood talking with a Gentleman in the corner of my Chamber, not regarding at all what I was doing : but he started suddenly, as if he had found some strange alteration in himself ; I asked him what he ailed ? I know not what ailes me, but I

4

find that I feel no more pain, methinks that a
pleasing kind of freshnesse, as it were a wet cold
Napkin did spread over my hand, which hath taken
away the inflammation that tormented me before ; I
replied, since that you feel already so good an effect
of my medicament, I advise you to cast away all
your Plaisters, onely keep the wound clean, and in a
moderate temper 'twixt heat and cold. This was
presently reported to the Duke of *Buckingham*,
and a little after to the King [James I.], who were
both very curious to know the issue of the businesse,
which was, that after dinner I took the garter out
of the water, and put it to dry before a great fire ; it
was scarce dry, but Mr *Howels* servant came running [and told me], that his Master felt as much burning as ever he had done, if not more, for the heat
was such, as if his hand were betwixt coales of fire :
I answered, that although that had happened at
present, yet he should find ease in a short time ; for
I knew the reason of this new accident, and I would
provide accordingly, for his Master should be free
from that inflammation, it may be, before he could
possibly return unto him : but in case he found no
ease, I wished him to come presently back again,
if not he might forbear coming. Thereupon he
went, and at the instant I did put again the garter
into the water ; thereupon he found his Master
without any pain at all. To be brief, there was
no sense of pain afterward : but within five or
six dayes the wounds were cicatrized, and entirely
healed." [1]

Sir KENELM proceeds, in this discourse, to relate

[1] *Ibid.*, pp. 7–11.

FIG. 16.

JAMES HOWELL, from an engraved Portrait by CLAUDE MELAN and
ABRAHAM BOSSE.

(By permission of the British Museum.   Photo by Donald Macbeth, London.)

that he obtained the secret of the Powder from a
Carmelite who had learnt it in the East. Sir
KENELM says that he told it only to King JAMES and
his celebrated physician, Sir THEODORE MAYERNE
(1573–1655). The latter disclosed it to the Duke of
MAYERNE, whose surgeon sold the secret to various
persons, until ultimately, as Sir KENELM remarks, it
became known to every country barber. However,
DIGBY's real connection with the Powder has been
questioned. In an Appendix to Dr NATHANAEL
HIGHMORE's (1613–1685) *The History of Generation*,
published in 1651, entitled *A Discourse of the Cure
of Wounds by Sympathy*, the Powder is referred
to as Sir GILBERT TALBOT's Powder ; nor does it
appear to have been DIGBY who brought the claims
of the Sympathetic Powder before the notice of
the then recently-formed Royal Society, although
he was a by no means inactive member of the
Society. HIGHMORE, however, in the Appendix to
the work referred to above, does refer to DIGBY's
reputed cure of HOWELL's wounds already mentioned ; and after the publication of DIGBY's *Discourse* the Powder became generally known as
Sir KENELM DIGBY's Sympathetic Powder. As
such it is referred to in an advertisement appended
to *Wit and Drollery* (1661) by the bookseller,
NATHANAEL BROOK.[1]

---

[1] This advertisement is as follows : " These are to give
notice, that Sir *Kenelme Digbies* Sympathetical Powder pre-
par'd by Promethean fire, curing all green wounds that come
within the compass of a Remedy ; and likewise the Tooth-ache
infallibly in a very short time : Is to be had at Mr *Nathanael
Brook's* at the Angel in *Cornhil.*"

The belief in cure by sympathy, however, is much older than DIGBY's or TALBOT's Sympathetic Powder. PARACELSUS described an ointment consisting essentially of the moss on the skull of a man who had died a violent death, combined with boar's and bear's fat, burnt worms, dried boar's brain, red sandal-wood and mummy, which was used to cure (?) wounds in a similar manner, being applied to the weapon with which the hurt had been inflicted. With reference to this ointment, readers will probably recall the passage in SCOTT's *Lay of the Last Minstrel* (canto 3, stanza 23), respecting the magical cure of WILLIAM of DELORAINE's wound by " the Ladye of Branksome " :—

> " She drew the splinter from the wound
>   And with a charm she stanch'd the blood ;
> She bade the gash be cleans'd and bound :
>   No longer by his couch she stood ;
> But she had ta'en the broken lance,
>   And washed it from the clotted gore
>   And salved the splinter o'er and o'er.
> William of Deloraine, in trance,
>   Whene'er she turned it round and round,
>   Twisted as if she gall'd his wound.
>   Then to her maidens she did say
>   That he should be whole man and sound
>   Within the course of a night and day.
> Full long she toil'd ; for she did rue
> Mishap to friend so stout and true."

FRANCIS BACON (1561–1626) writes of sympathetic cures as follows :—" It is constantly Received, and Avouched, that the *Anointing* of the *Weapon*, that maketh the *Wound*, wil heale the *Wound* it selfe. In this *Experiment*, upon the Relation of *Men* of *Credit*,

Effigies Nathanaelis Highmory in Medicina Doctoris, ætatis suæ 63. ano Dom: 1677.

A. Blooteling f.

FIG. 17.

NATHANAEL HIGHMORE, M.D., from an engraved Portrait by A. BLOOTELING.

(By permission of the British Museum. Photo by Donald Macbeth, London.)

(though my selfe, as yet, am not fully inclined to beleeve it,) you shal note the *Points* following ; First, the *Ointment* . . . is made of Divers *ingredients* ; whereof the Strangest and Hardest to come by, are the *Mosse* upon the *Skull* of a *dead Man, Vnburied* ; And the *Fats* of a *Boare*, and a *Beare*, killed in the *Act* of *Generation*. These Two last I could easily suspect to be prescribed as a Starting Hole ; That if the *Experiment* proved not, it mought be pretended, that the *Beasts* were not killed in due Time ; For as for the *Mosse*, it is certain there is great Quantity of it in *Ireland*, upon *Slain Bodies*, laid on *Heaps, Vnburied*. The other *Ingredients* are, the *Bloud-Stone* in *Powder*, and some other *Things*, which seeme to have a *Vertue* to *Stanch Bloud* ; As also the *Mosse* hath. . . . Secondly, the same *kind* of *Ointment*, applied to the Hurt it selfe, worketh not the *Effect* ; but onely applied to the *Weapon*. . . . . Fourthly, it may be applied to the *Weapon*, though the *Party Hurt* be at a great *Distance*. Fifthly, it seemeth the *Imagination* of the Party, to be *Cured*, is not needfull to Concurre ; For it may be done without the knowledge of the *Party Wounded* ; And thus much hath been tried, that the *Ointment* (for *Experiments* sake,) hath been wiped off the *Weapon*, without the knowledge of the *Party Hurt,* and presently the *Party Hurt*, hath been in great *Rage* of *Paine*, till the *Weapon* was *Reannointed*. Sixthly, it is affirmed, that if you cannot get the *Weapon*, yet if you put an *Instrument* of *Iron*, or *Wood*, resembling the *Weapon*, into the *Wound*, whereby it bleedeth, the *Annointing* of that *Instrument* will serve, and work the *Effect*. This I doubt should be a Device, to keep this strange

Forme of *Cure*, in Request, and Use ; Because many times you cannot come by the *Weapon* it selve. Seventhly, the *Wound* be at first *Washed clean* with *White Wine* or the *Parties* own *Water* ; And then bound up close in *Fine Linen* and no more *Dressing* renewed, till it be *whole*." [1]

Owing to the demand for making this ointment, quite a considerable trade was done in skulls from Ireland upon which moss had grown owing to their exposure to the atmosphere, high prices being obtained for fine specimens.

The idea underlying the belief in the efficacy of sympathetic remedies, namely, that by acting on part of a thing or on a symbol of it, one thereby acts magically on the whole or the thing symbolised, is the root-idea of all magic, and is of extreme antiquity. DIGBY and others, however, tried to give a natural explanation to the supposed efficacy of the Powder. They argued that particles of the blood would ascend from the bloody cloth or weapon, only coming to rest when they had reached their natural home in the wound from which they had originally issued. These particles would carry with them the more volatile part of the vitriol, which would effect a cure more readily than when combined with the grosser part of the vitriol. In the days when there was hardly any knowledge of chemistry and physics, this theory no doubt bore every semblance of truth. In passing, however, it is interesting to note that DIGBY's *Discourse* called forth a reply from J. F.

---

[1] FRANCIS BACON : *Sylva Sylvarum: or, A Natural History* . . . *Published after the Authors death* . . . *The sixt Edition* . . . (1651), p. 217.

Honble Francisc° Bacon° Baro de Veru
lam. Vice-Comes S.^{cti} Albani, mortuus 9 Aprilis
Anno Dni 1626. Anno͠q Ætat 66.

FIG. 18.
FRANCIS BACON, from the Frontispiece to his *Sylva Sylvarum*
(6th edition, 1651).

HELVETIUS (or SCHWEITZER, 1625–1709), physician to the Prince of Orange, who afterwards became celebrated as an alchemist who had achieved the *magnum opus*.[1]

Writing of the Sympathetic Powder, Professor DE MORGAN wittily argues that it must have been quite efficacious. He says : " The directions were to keep the wound clean and cool, and to take care of diet, rubbing the salve on the knife or sword. If we remember the dreadful notions upon drugs which prevailed, both as to quantity and quality, we shall readily see that any way of *not* dressing the wound would have been useful. If the physicians had taken the hint, had been careful of diet, *etc.*, and had poured the little barrels of medicine down the throat of a practicable doll, *they* would have had their magical cures as well as the surgeons." [2] As Dr PETTIGREW has pointed out,[3] Nature exhibits very remarkable powers in effecting the healing of wounds by adhesion, when her processes are not impeded. In fact, many cases have been recorded in which noses, ears, and fingers severed from the body have been re-joined thereto, merely by washing the parts, placing them in close continuity, and allowing the natural powers of the body to effect the healing. Moreover, in spite of BACON's remarks on this point, the effect of the imagination of the patient, who was

[1] See my *Alchemy : Ancient and Modern* (1911), §§ 63–67.

[2] Professor AUGUSTUS DE MORGAN : *A Budget of Paradoxes* (1872), p. 66.

[3] THOMAS JOSEPH PETTIGREW, F.R.S.: *On Superstitions connected with the History and Practice of Medicine and Surgery* (1844), pp. 164–167.

usually not ignorant that a sympathetic cure was to be attempted, must be taken into account; for, without going to the excesses of " Christian Science " in this respect, the fact must be recognised that the state of the mind exercises a powerful effect on the natural forces of the body, and a firm faith is undoubtedly helpful in effecting the cure of any sort of ill.

VI

THE BELIEF IN TALISMANS

THE word " talisman " is derived from the Arabic
" tilsam," " a magical image," through the plural
form " tilsamén." This Arabic word is itself probably derived from the Greek τέλεσμα in its late
meaning of " a religious mystery " or " consecrated
object ". The term is often employed to designate
amulets in general, but, correctly speaking, it has a
more restricted and special significance. A talisman
may be defined briefly as an astrological or other
symbol expressive of the influence and power of one
of the planets, engraved on a sympathetic stone or
metal (or inscribed on specially prepared parchment)
under the auspices of this planet.

Before proceeding to an account of the preparation
of talismans proper, it will not be out of place to
notice some of the more interesting and curious of
other amulets. All sorts of substances have been
employed as charms, sometimes of a very unpleasant
nature, such as dried toads. Generally, however,
amulets consist of stones, herbs, or passages from
Sacred Writings written on paper. This latter class
are sometimes called " characts," as an example of
which may be mentioned the Jewish phylacteries.

Every precious stone was supposed to exercise its own peculiar virtue; for instance, amber was regarded as a good remedy for throat troubles, and agate was thought to preserve from snake-bites. ELIHU RICH [1] gives a very full list of stones and their supposed virtues. Each sign of the zodiac was supposed to have its own particular stone [2] (as shown in the annexed table), and hence the superstitious though not inartistic custom of wearing one's birth-

Sign of the Zodiac.	Astro-logical Symbol.	Month (commencing about the 21st of preceding month).	Stone.
Aries, the Ram	♈	April	Sardonyx.
Taurus, the Bull	♉	May	Cornelian.
Gemini, the Twins	♊	June	Topaz.
Cancer, the Crab	♋	July	Chalcedony.
Leo, the Lion	♌	August	Jasper.
Virgo, the Virgin	♍	September	Emerald.
Libra, the Balance	♎	October	Beryl.
Scorpio, the Scorpion	♏	November	Amethyst.
Sagittarius, the Archer	♐	December	Hyacinth (=Sapphire).
Capricorn, the Goat	♑	January	Chrysoprase.
Aquarius, the Water-bearer	♒	February	Crystal.
Pisces, the Fishes	♓	March	Sapphire (=Lapis lazuli).

[1] ELIHU RICH: *The Occult Sciences* (*Encyclopædia Metropolitana*, 1855), pp. 348 *et seq.*

[2] With regard to these stones, however, there is much confusion and difference of opinion. The arrangement adopted in the table here given is that of CORNELIUS AGRIPPA (*Occult Philosophy*, bk. ii.). A comparatively recent work, esteemed

stone for " luck ".   The belief in the occult powers
of certain stones is by no means non-existent at the
present day ; for even in these enlightened times
there are not wanting those who fear the beautiful
opal, and put their faith in the virtues of New Zealand
green-stone.

Certain herbs, culled at favourable conjunctions of
the planets and worn as amulets, were held to be very
efficacious against various diseases.   Precious stones
and metals were also taken internally for the same

by modern occultists, namely, *The Light of Egypt, or the Science
of the Soul and the Stars* (1889), gives the following scheme :—

♈ =Amethyst. ♋=Emerald. ♎=Diamond. ♑ =Onyx (Chalce-
                                                                                dony).
♉ =Agate.   ♌=Ruby.   ♏=Topaz.   ♒=Sapphire (sky-
                                                                                blue).
♊ =Beryl.   ♍ =Jasper.   ♐ =Carbuncle. ♓ =Chrysolite.

Common superstitious opinion regarding birth-stones, as
reflected, for example, in the " lucky birth charms " exhibited
in the windows of the jewellers' shops, considerably diverges
in this matter from the views of both these authorities.   The
usual scheme is as follows :—

Jan. =Garnet.	May =Emerald.	Sept.=Sapphire.
Feb. =Amethyst.	June=Agate.	Oct. =Opal.
Mar. =Bloodstone.	July =Ruby.	Nov. =Topaz.
Apr. =Diamond.	Aug. =Sardonyx.	Dec. =Turquoise.

The bloodstone is frequently assigned either to Aries or
Scorpio, owing to its symbolical connection with Mars ; and
the opal to Cancer, which in astrology is the constellation of
the moon.

Confusion is rendered still worse by the fact that the ancients,
whilst in some cases using the same names as ourselves, applied
them to different stones ; thus their " hyacinth " is our
" sapphire," whilst their " sapphire " is our " lapis lazuli ".

purpose—" remedies " which in certain cases must have proved exceedingly harmful. One theory put forward for the supposed medical value of amulets was the Doctrine of Effluvia. This theory supposes the amulets to give off vapours or effluvia which penetrate into the body and effect a cure. It is, of course, true that certain herbs, *etc.*, might, under the heat of the body, give off such effluvia, but the theory on the whole is manifestly absurd. The Doctrine of Signatures, which we have already encountered in our excursions,[1] may also be mentioned in this connection as a complementary and equally untenable hypothesis.

According to ELIHU RICH,[2] the following were the commonest Egyptian amulets :—

1. Those inscribed with the figure of *Serapis*, used to preserve against evils inflicted by earth.

2. Figure of *Canopus*, against evil by water.

3. Figure of a *hawk*, against evil from the air.

4. Figure of an *asp*, against evil by fire.

PARACELSUS believed there to be much occult virtue in an alloy of the seven chief metals, which he called *Electrum*. Certain definite proportions of these metals had to be taken, and each was to be added during a favourable conjunction of the planets. From this electrum he supposed that valuable amulets and magic mirrors could be prepared.

A curious and ancient amulet for the cure of various diseases, particularly the ague, was a triangle formed of the letters of the word " Abracadabra." The usual form was that shown in fig. 19, and that

---

[1] See " Medicine and Magic."   [2] *Op. cit.*, p. 343.

shown in fig. 20 was also known.   The origin of this magical word is lost in obscurity.

The belief in the horn as a powerful amulet, especially prevalent in Italy, where is it the custom of the common people to make the sign of the *mano cornuto* to avoid the consequence of the dreaded

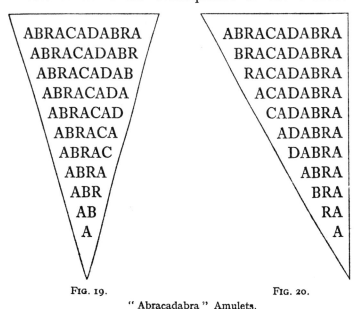

FIG. 19.   FIG. 20.

" Abracadabra " Amulets.

jettatore or evil eye, can be traced to the fact that the horn was the symbol of the Goddess of the Moon. Probably the belief in the powers of the horse-shoe [1] had a similar origin.   Indeed, it seems likely that not only this, but most other amulets, like talismans proper—as will appear below,—were originally designed as appeals to gods and other powerful spiritual beings.

[1] See FREDERICK T. ELWORTHY'S *Horns of Honour* (1900), especially pp. 56 *et seq.*

To turn our attention, however, to the art of preparing talismans proper : I may remark at the outset
that it was necessary for the talisman to be prepared
by one's own self—a task by no means easy as a rule.
Indeed, the right mental attitude of the occultist was
insisted upon as essential to the operation.

As to the various signs to be engraven on the
talismans, various authorities differ, though there are
certain points connected with the art of talismanic
magic on which they all agree. It so happened that
the ancients were acquainted with seven metals and
seven planets (including the sun and moon as planets),
and the days of the week are also seven. It was
concluded, therefore, that there was some occult connection between the planets, metals, and days of the
week. Each of the seven days of the week was
supposed to be under the auspices of the spirits of
one of the planets ; so also was the generation in the
womb of Nature of each of the seven chief metals.

In the following table are shown these particulars
in detail :—

1. Planet.	2. Symbol.	3. Day of Week.	4. Metal.	5. Colour.
Sun .	☉	Sunday	Gold	Gold or yellow.
Moon .	☽	Monday	Silver	Silver or white.
Mars .	♂	Tuesday	Iron	Red.
Mercury	☿	Wednesday	[1]Mercury	Mixed colours or purple.
Jupiter	♃	Thursday	Tin	Violet or blue.
Venus .	♀	Friday	Copper	Turquoise or green.
Saturn .	♄	Saturday	Lead	Black.

[1] Used in the form of a solid amalgam for talismans.

Consequently, the metal of which a talisman was to be made, and also the time of its preparation, had to be chosen with due regard to the planet under which it was to be prepared.[1] The power of such a talisman was thought to be due to the genie of this planet—a talisman, was, in fact, a silent evocation of an astral spirit. Examples of the belief that a genie can be bound up in an amulet in some way are afforded

[1] In this connection a rather surprising discovery made by Mr W. Gorn Old (see his *A Manual of Occultism*, 1911, pp. 7 and 8) must be mentioned. The ancient Chaldeans appear invariably to have enumerated the planets in the following order: Saturn, Jupiter, Mars, Sun, Venus, Mercury, Moon—which order was adopted by the mediæval astrologers. Let us commence with the Sun in the above sequence, and write down every third planet; we then have—

Sun	.	.	.	. Sunday.
Moon	.	.	.	. Monday.
Mars	.	.	.	. Tuesday.
Mercury	.	.	.	. Wednesday.
Jupiter	.	.	.	. Thursday.
Venus	.	.	.	. Friday.
Saturn	.	.	.	. Saturday.

That is to say, we have the planets in the order in which they were supposed to rule over the days of the week. This is, perhaps, not so surprising, because it seems probable that, each day being first divided into twenty-four hours, it was assumed that the planets ruled for one hour in turn, in the order first mentioned above. Each day was then named after the planet which ruled during its first hour. It will be found that if we start with the Sun and write down every twenty-fourth planet, the result is exactly the same as if we write down every third. But Mr Old points out further, doing so by means of a diagram which seems to be rather cumbersome, that if we start with Saturn in the first place, and write down every fifth planet, and then for each planet substitute the

by the story of ALADDIN's lamp and ring and other stories in the *Thousand and One Nights*. Sometimes the talismanic signs were engraved on precious stones, sometimes they were inscribed on parchment ; in both cases the same principle held good, the nature of the stone chosen, or the colour of the ink employed, being that in correspondence with the planet under whose auspices the talisman was prepared.

All the instruments employed in the art had to be specially prepared and consecrated. Special robes had to be worn, perfumes and incense burnt, and invocations, conjurations, *etc.*, recited, all of which depended on the planet ruling the operation. A metal over which it was supposed to rule, we then have these metals arranged in descending order of atomic weights, thus :—

Saturn	.	.	.	.	Lead (=207).
Mercury	.	.	.	.	Mercury (=200).
Sun	.	.	.	.	Gold (=197).
Jupiter	.	.	.	.	Tin (=119).
Moon	.	.	.	.	Silver (=108).
Venus	.	.	.	.	Copper (=64).
Mars	.	.	.	.	Iron (=56).

Similarly we can, starting from any one of these orders, pass to the other two. The fact is a very surprising one, because the ancients could not possibly have been acquainted with the atomic weights of the metals, and, it is important to note, the order of the densities of these metals, which might possibly have been known to them, is by no means the same as the order of their atomic weights. Whether the fact indicates a real relationship between the planets and the metals, or whether there is some other explanation, I am not prepared to say. Certainly some explanation is needed : to say that the fact is mere coincidence is unsatisfactory, seeing that the odds against, not merely this, but any such regularity occurring by chance — as calculated by the mathematical theory of probability—are 119 to 1.

description of a few typical talismans in detail will
not here be out of place.

In *The Key of Solomon the King* (translated by
S. L. M. Mathers, 1889)[1] are described five, six, or

---

[1] The *Clavicula Salomonis*, or *Key of Solomon the King*, consists mainly of an elaborate ritual for the evocation of the
various planetary spirits, in which process the use of talismans
or pentacles plays a prominent part. It is claimed to be a
work of white magic, but, inasmuch as it, like other old books
making the same claim, gives descriptions of a pentacle for
causing ruin, destruction, and death, and another for causing
earthquakes—to give only two examples,—the distinction
between black and white magic, which we shall no doubt
encounter again in later excursions, appears to be somewhat
arbitrary.

Regarding the authorship of the work, Mr Mathers, trans-
lator and editor of the first printed copy of the book, says,
" I see no reason to doubt the tradition which assigns the
authorship of the ' Key ' to King Solomon." If this view be
accepted, however, it is abundantly evident that the *Key* as
it stands at present (in which we find S. John quoted, and
mention made of SS. Peter and Paul) must have received
some considerable alterations and additions at the hands of
later editors. But even if we are compelled to assign the
Clavicula Salomonis in its present form to the fourteenth or
fifteenth century, we must, I think, allow that it was based
upon traditions of the past, and, of course, the possibility
remains that it might have been based upon some earlier work.
With regard to the antiquity of the planetary sigils, Mr
Mathers notes " that, among the Gnostic talismans in the
British Museum, there is a ring of copper with the sigils of
Venus, which are exactly the same as those given by mediæval
writers on magic."

In spite of the absurdity of its claims, viewed in the light of
modern knowledge, the *Clavicula Salomonis* exercised a considerable influence in the past, and is to be regarded as one of
the chief sources of mediæval ceremonial magic. Historically
speaking, therefore, it is a book of no little importance.

5

seven talismans for each planet. Each of these was
supposed to have its own peculiar virtues, and many
of them are stated to be of use in the evocation of
spirits. The majority of them consist of a central
design encircled by a verse of Hebrew Scripture.

FIG. 21.

The First Pentacle of the Sun, from *Clavicula Salomonis*.

The central designs are of a varied character, generally
geometrical figures and Hebrew letters or words, or
magical characters. Five of these talismans are here
portrayed, the first three described differing from
the above. The translations of the Hebrew verses,
etc., given below are due to Mr MATHERS.

The First Pentacle of the Sun.—" The Countenance
of Shaddaï the Almighty, at Whose aspect all creatures

obey, and the Angelic Spirits do reverence on bended knees."   About the face is the name " El Shaddaï ". Around is written in Latin : " Behold His face and form by Whom all things were made, and Whom all creatures obey " (see fig. 21).

FIG. 22.
The Fifth Pentacle of Mars, from *Clavicula Salomonis*.

The Fifth Pentacle of Mars.—" Write thou this Pentacle upon virgin parchment or paper because it is terrible unto the Demons, and at its sight and aspect they will obey thee, for they cannot resist its presence."   The design is a Scorpion,[1] around which the word Hvl is repeated.   The Hebrew versicle

[1] In astrology the zodiacal sign of the Scorpion is the " night house " of the planet Mars.

is from *Psalm* xci. 13 : " Thou shalt go upon the
lion and adder, the young lion and the dragon shalt
thou tread under thy feet " (see fig. 22).

The Third Pentacle of the Moon.—" This being
duly borne with thee when upon a journey, if it be

FIG. 23.
The Third Pentacle of the Moon, from *Clavicula Salomonis*.

properly made, serveth against all attacks by night,
and against every kind of danger and peril by Water."
The design consists of a hand and sleeved forearm
(this occurs on three other moon talismans), together
with the Hebrew names Aub and Vevaphel. The
versicle is from *Psalm* xl. 13 : ' Be pleased O IHVH
to deliver me, O IHVH make haste to help me " (see
fig. 23).

The Third Pentacle of Venus.—" This, if it be only shown unto any person, serveth to attract love. Its Angel Monachiel should be invoked in the day and hour of Venus, at one o'clock or at eight." The design consists of two triangles joined at their apices,

FIG. 24.

The Third Pentacle of Venus, from *Clavicula Salomonis*.

with the following names—IHVH, Adonai, Ruach, Achides, Ægalmiel, Monachiel, and Degaliel. The versicle is from *Genesis* i. 28 : " And the Elohim blessed them, and the Elohim said unto them, Be ye fruitful, and multiply, and replenish the earth, and subdue it " (see fig. 24).

The Third Pentacle of Mercury.—" This serves to invoke the Spirits subject unto Mercury ; and

especially those who are written in this Pentacle."
The design consists of crossed lines and magical
characters of Mercury. Around are the names of
the angels, Kokaviel, Ghedoriah, Savaniah, and
Chokmahiel (see fig. 25).

FIG. 25.
The Third Pentacle of Mercury, from *Clavicula Salomonis*.

CORNELIUS AGRIPPA, in his *Three Books of Occult
Philosophy*, describes another interesting system of
talismans. FRANCIS BARRETT'S *Magus, or Celestial
Intelligencer*, a well-known occult work published
in the first year of the nineteenth century, I may
mention, copies AGRIPPA'S system of talismans, without acknowledgment, almost word for word. To
each of the planets is assigned a magic square or

table, *i.e.* a square composed of numbers so arranged that the sum of each row or column is always the same. For example, the table for Mars is as follows :—

11	24	7	20	3
4	12	25	8	16
17	5	13	21	9
10	18	1	14	22
23	6	19	2	15

It will be noticed that every number from 1 up to the highest possible occurs once, and that no number occurs twice. It will also be seen that the sum of each row and of each column is always 65. Similar squares can be constructed containing any square number of figures, and it is, indeed, by no means surprising that the remarkable properties of such " magic squares," before these were explained mathematically, gave rise to the belief that they had some occult significance and virtue. From the magic squares can be obtained certain numbers which are said to be the numbers of the planets ; their orderliness, we are told, reflects the order of the heavens, and from a consideration of them the magical properties of the planets which they represent can be arrived at. For example, in the above table the number of rows of numbers is 5. The total number of numbers in the table is the square of this number, namely, 25, which is also the greatest number in the table. The sum of any row or column is 65. And, finally, the sum of all the numbers is the product of the number of rows (namely, 5) and the sum of any row (namely, 65), *i.e.* 325. These numbers, namely, 5, 25, 65, and

325, are the numbers of Mars. Sets of numbers for the other planets are obtained in exactly the same manner.[1]

Now to each planet is assigned an Intelligence or good spirit, and an Evil Spirit or demon ; and the names of these spirits are related to certain of the numbers of the planets. The other numbers are also connected with holy and magical Hebrew names. AGRIPPA, and BARRETT copying him, gives the following table of " names answering to the numbers of Mars " :—

5.	He, the letter of the holy name.	ה
25.		יהי
65.	Adonai.	אדני
325.	Graphiel, the Intelligence of Mars.	גראפיאל
325.	Barzabel, the Spirit of Mars.	ברעאבאל

Similar tables are given for the other planets. The numbers can be derived from the names by regarding the Hebrew letters of which they are composed as numbers, in which case א (Aleph) to ט (Teth) represent the units 1 to 9 in order, י (Jod) to צ (Tzade) the tens 10 to 90 in order, ק (Koph) to ת (Tau) the hundreds 100 to 400, whilst the hundreds 500 to 900 are represented by special terminal forms of certain of the Hebrew letters.[2] It is evident that

---

[1] Readers acquainted with mathematics will notice that if n is the number of rows in such a " magic square," the other numbers derived as above will be n^2, $\frac{1}{2}n(n^2+1)$, and $\frac{1}{2}n^2(n^2+1)$. This can readily be proved by the laws of arithmetical progressions. Rather similar but more complicated and less uniform " magic squares " are attributed to PARACELSUS.

[2] It may be noticed that this makes ברעאבאל equal to 326, one unit too much. Possibly an Aleph should be omitted.

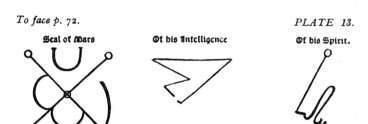

Seal of Mars   Of his Intelligence   Of his Spirit.

FIG. 26.   FIG. 27.   FIG. 28.

The Seals of Mars, his Intelligence, and his Spirit, from BARRETT'S
Magus (1801).

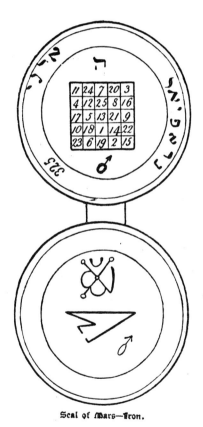

Seal of Mars—Iron.

FIG. 29.

The Talisman of Mars, from BARRETT'S *Magus.*

no little wasted ingenuity must have been employed
in working all this out.

Each planet has its own seal or signature, as well
as the signature of its intelligence and the signature
of its demon. These signatures were supposed to
represent the characters of the planets' intelligences
and demons respectively. The signature of Mars is
shown in fig. 26, that of its intelligence in fig. 27,
and that of its demon in fig. 28.

These various details were inscribed on the talismans—each of which was supposed to confer its
own peculiar benefits—as follows : On one side
must be engraved the proper magic table and the
astrological sign of the planet, together with the
highest planetary number, the sacred names corresponding to the planet, and the name of the intelligence of the planet, but not the name of its demon.
On the other side must be engraved the seals of the
planet and of its intelligence, and also the astrological
sign. BARRETT says, regarding the demons : [1] " It is
to be understood that the intelligences are the pre-
siding good angels that are set over the planets ; but
that the spirits or dæmons, with their names, seals,
or characters, are never inscribed upon any Talisman,
except to execute any evil effect, and that they are
subject to the intelligences, or good spirits ; and
again, when the spirits and their characters are used,
it will be more conducive to the effect to add some
divine name appropriate to that effect which we
desire." Evil talismans can also be prepared, we
are informed, by using a metal antagonistic to the

[1] FRANCIS BARRETT: *The Magus, or Celestial Intelligencer*
(1801), bk. i. p. 146.

signs engraved thereon. The complete talisman of
Mars is shown in fig. 29.

ALPHONSE LOUIS CONSTANT,[1] a famous French
occultist of the nineteenth century, who wrote under
the name of " ÉLIPHAS LÉVI," describes yet another
system of talismans. He says : " The Pentagram
must be always engraved on one side of the talisman,
with a circle for the Sun, a crescent for the Moon, a
winged caduceus for Mercury, a sword for Mars, a
G for Venus, a crown for Jupiter, and a scythe for
Saturn. The other side of the talisman should bear
the sign of Solomon, that is, the six-pointed star
formed by two interlaced triangles ; in the centre
there should be placed a human figure for the sun
talismans, a cup for those of the Moon, a dog's head
for those of Jupiter, a lion for those of Mars, a dove's
for those of Venus, a bull's or goat's for those of
Saturn. The names of the seven angels should be
added either in Hebrew, Arabic, or magic characters
similar to those of the alphabets of Trimethius. The
two triangles of Solomon may be replaced by the
double cross of Ezekiel's wheels, this being found on
a great number of ancient pentacles. All objects of
this nature, whether in metals or in precious stones,
should be carefully wrapped in silk satchels of a
colour analogous to the spirit of the planet, perfumed
with the perfumes of the corresponding day, and
preserved from all impure looks and touches."[2]

ÉLIPHAS LÉVI, following PYTHAGORAS and many

---

[1] For a biographical and critical account of this extraordinary personage and his views, see Mr A. E. WAITE's *The
Mysteries of Magic : a Digest of the Writings of* ÉLIPHAS LÉVI
(1897).　　　　　[2] *Op. cit.*, p. 204.

Fig. 30.

The Pentagram embellished according to
Éliphas Lévi.

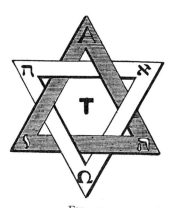

Fig. 31.

The Hexagram, or Seal of Solomon, embellished
according to Éliphas Lévi.

of the mediæval magicians, regarded the pentagram, or five-pointed star, as an extremely powerful pentacle. According to him, if with one horn in the ascendant it is the sign of the microcosm—Man. With two horns in the ascendant, however, it is the sign of the Devil, " the accursed Goat of Mendes," and an instrument of black magic. We can, indeed, trace some faint likeness between the pentagram and the outline form of a man, or of a goat's head, according to whether it has one or two horns in the ascendant respectively, which resemblances may account for this idea. Fig. 30 shows the pentagram embellished with other symbols according to ÉLIPHAS LÉVI, whilst fig. 31 shows his embellished form of the six-pointed star, or Seal of SOLOMON. This, he says, is " the sign of the Macrocosmos, but is less powerful than the Pentagram, the microcosmic sign," thus contradicting PYTHAGORAS, who, as we have seen, regarded the pentagram as the sign of the Macrocosm. ÉLIPHAS LÉVI asserts that he attempted the evocation of the spirit of APOLLONIUS of Tyana in London on 24th July 1854, by the aid of a pentagram and other magical apparatus and ritual, apparently with success, if we may believe his word. But he sensibly suggests that probably the apparition which appeared was due to the effect of the ceremonies on his own imagination, and comes to the conclusion that such magical experiments are injurious to health.[1]

Magical rings were prepared on the same principle as were talismans. Says CORNELIUS AGRIPPA: " The manner of making these kinds of Magical Rings is this,

[1] *Op. cit.*, pp. 446–450.

viz.: When any Star ascends fortunately, with the fortunate aspect or conjunction of the Moon, we must take a stone and herb that is under that Star, and make a ring of the metal that is suitable to this Star, and in it fasten the stone, putting the herb or root under it—not omitting the inscriptions of images, names, and characters, as also the proper suffumigations. . . ." [1] SOLOMON'S ring was supposed to have been possessed of remarkable occult virtue. Says JOSEPHUS (*c*. A.D. 37–100): " God also enabled him [SOLOMON] to learn that skill which expels demons, which is a science useful and sanative to men. He composed such incantations also by which distempers are alleviated. And he left behind him the manner of using exorcisms, by which they drive away demons, so that they never return ; and this method of cure is of great force unto this day ; for I have seen a certain man of my own country, whose name was Eleazar, releasing people that were demoniacal in the presence of Vespasian, and his sons, and his captains, and the whole multitude of his soldiers. The manner of the cure was this ; he put a ring that had under the seal a root of one of those sorts mentioned by Solomon, to the nostrils of the demoniac, after which he drew out the demon through his nostrils : and when the man fell down immediately, he abjured him to return unto him no more, making still mention of Solomon, and reciting the incantations which he composed." [2]

---

[1] H. C. AGRIPPA: *Occult Philosophy*, bk. i. chap. xlvii. (WHITEHEAD'S edition, pp. 141 and 142).

[2] FLAVIUS JOSEPHUS: *The Antiquities of the Jews* (trans. by W. WHISTON), bk. viii. chap. ii., § 5 (45) to (47).

Enough has been said already to indicate the general nature of talismanic magic. No one could maintain otherwise than that much of it is pure nonsense; but the subject should not, therefore, be dismissed as valueless, or lacking significance. It is past belief that amulets and talismans should have been believed in for so long unless they *appeared* to be productive of some of the desired results, though these may have been due to forces quite other than those which were supposed to be operative. Indeed, it may be said that there has been no widely held superstition which does not embody some truth, like some small specks of gold hidden in an uninviting mass of quartz. As the poet BLAKE put it: " Everything possible to be believ'd is an image of truth "; [1] and the attempt may here be made to extract the gold of truth from the quartz of superstition concerning talismanic magic. For this purpose the various theories regarding the supposed efficacy of talismans must be examined.

Two of these theories have already been noted, but the doctrine of effluvia admittedly applied only to a certain class of amulets, and, I think, need not be seriously considered. The " astral-spirit theory " (as it may be called), in its ancient form at any rate, is equally untenable to-day. The discoveries of new planets and new metals seem destructive of the belief that there can be any occult connection between planets, metals, and the days of the week, although the curious fact discovered by Mr OLD, to which I have referred (footnote, p. 63), assuredly demands an explanation, and a certain validity may, perhaps,

[1] " Proverbs of Hell " (*The Marriage of Heaven and Hell*).

be allowed to astrological symbolism. As concerns the belief in the existence of what may be called (although the term is not a very happy one) " discarnate spirits," however, the matter, in view of the modern investigation of spiritistic and other abnormal psychical phenomena, stands in a different position. There can, indeed, be little doubt that very many of the phenomena observed at spiritistic seances come under the category of deliberate fraud, and an even larger number, perhaps, can be explained on the theory of the subconscious self. I think, however, that the evidence goes to show that there is a residuum of phenomena which can only be explained by the operation, in some way, of discarnate intelligences.[1] Psychical research may be said to have supplied the modern world with the evidence of the existence of discarnate personalities, and of their operation on the material plane, which the ancient world lacked. But so far as our present subject is concerned, all the evidence obtainable goes to show that the phenomena in question only take place in the presence of what is called " a medium "—a person of peculiar nervous or psychical organisation. That this is the case, moreover, appears to be the general belief of spiritists on the subject. In the sense, then, in which " a talisman " connotes a material object of such a nature that by its aid the powers of discarnate intel-

[1] The publications of The Society for Psychical Research, and FREDERICK MYERS' monumental work on *Human Personality and its Survival of Bodily Death,* should be specially consulted. I have attempted a brief discussion of modern spiritualism and psychical research in my *Matter, Spirit, and the Cosmos* (1910), chap. ii.

ligences may become operative on material things,
we might apply the term " talisman " to the nervous
system of a medium : but then that would be the only
talisman.   Consequently, even if one is prepared to
admit the whole of modern spiritistic theory, nothing
is thereby gained towards a belief in talismans, and
no light is shed upon the subject.

Another theory concerning talismans which com-
mended itself to many of the old occult philosophers,
PARACELSUS for instance, is what may be called the
" occult force " theory.   This theory assumes the
existence of an occult mental force, a force capable
of being exerted by the human will, apart from its
usual mode of operation by means of the body.   It
was believed to be possible to concentrate this mental
energy and infuse it into some suitable medium,
with the production of a talisman, which was thus
regarded as a sort of accumulator for mental energy.
The theory seems a fantastic one to modern thought,
though, in view of the many startling phenomena
brought to light by psychical research, it is not
advisable to be too positive regarding the limitations
of the powers of the human mind.   However, I
think we shall find the element of truth in the otherwise absurd belief in talismans by means of what
may be called, not altogether fancifully perhaps, a
transcendental interpretation of this " occult force "
theory.   I suggest, that is, that when a believer makes
a talisman, the transference of the occult energy is
ideal, not actual ; that the power, believed to reside
in the talisman itself, is the power due to the reflex
action of the believer's mind.   The power of what
transcendentalists call " the imagination " cannot be

denied; for example, no one can deny that a man with a firm conviction that such a success will be achieved by him, or such a danger avoided, will be far more likely to gain his desire, other conditions being equal, than one of a pessimistic turn of mind. The mere conviction itself is a factor in success, or a factor in failure, according to its nature; and it seems likely that herein will be found a true explanation of the effects believed to be due to the power of the talisman.

On the other hand, however, we must beware of the exaggerations into which certain schools of thought have fallen in their estimates of the powers of the imagination. These exaggerations are particularly marked in the views which are held by many nowadays with regard to " faith-healing," although the " Christian Scientists " get out of the difficulty—at least to their own satisfaction—by ascribing their alleged cures to the Power of the Divine Mind, and not to the power of the individual mind.

Of course the real question involved in this " transcendental theory of talismans " as I may, perhaps, call it, is that of the operation of incarnate spirit on the plane of matter. This operation takes place only through the medium of the nervous system, and it has been suggested,[1] to avoid any violation of the law of the conservation of energy, that it is effected, not by the transference, as is sometimes supposed, of energy from the spiritual to the material plane, but merely by means of directive control over the expenditure of energy derived by the body from purely

[1] *Cf.* Sir OLIVER LODGE: *Life and Matter* (1907), especially chap. ix. ; and W. HIBBERT, F.I.C.: *Life and Energy* (1904).

physical sources, *e.g.* the latent chemical energy bound up in the food eaten and the oxygen breathed.

I am not sure that this theory really avoids the difficulty which it is intended to obviate ; [1] but it is at least an interesting one, and at any rate there may be modes in which the body, under the directive control of the spirit, may expend energy derived from the material plane, of which we know little or nothing. We have the testimony of many eminent authorities [2] to the phenomenon of the movement of physical objects without contact at spiritistic seances. It seems to me that the introduction of discarnate intelligences to explain this phenomenon is somewhat gratuitous—the psychic phenomena which yield evidence of the survival of human personality after bodily death are of a different character. For if we suppose this particular phenomenon to be due to discarnate spirits, we must, in view of what has been said concerning " mediums," conclude that the movements in question are not produced by these spirits *directly*, but through and by means of the nervous system of the medium present. Evidently, therefore, the means for the production of the phenomenon reside in the human nervous system (or, at any rate, in the peculiar nervous system of " mediums "), and all that is lacking is intelligence

[1] The subject is rather too technical to deal with here. I have discussed it elsewhere ; see " Thermo-Dynamical Objections to the Mechanical Theory of Life," *The Chemical News*, vol. cxii. pp. 271 *et seq.* (3rd December 1915).

[2] For instance, the well-known physicist, Sir W. F. BARRETT, F.R.S. (late Professor of Experimental Physics in The Royal College of Science for Ireland). See his *On the Threshold of a New World of Thought* (1908), § 10.

or initiative to use these means. This intelligence or initiative can surely be as well supplied by the sub-consciousness as by a discarnate intelligence. Consequently, it does not seem unreasonable to suppose that equally remarkable phenomena may have been produced by the aid of talismans in the days when these were believed in, and may be produced to-day, if one has sufficient faith—that is to say, produced by man when in the peculiar condition of mind brought about by the intense belief in the power of a talisman. And here it should be noted that the term " talisman " may be applied to any object (or doctrine) that is believed to possess peculiar power or efficacy. In this fact, I think, is to be found the peculiar danger of erroneous doctrines which promise extraordinary benefits, here and now on the material plane, to such as believe in them. Remarkable results may follow an intense belief in such doctrines, which, whilst having no connection whatever with their accuracy, being proportional only to the intensity with which they are held, cannot do otherwise than confirm the believer in the validity of his beliefs, though these may be in every way highly fantastic and erroneous. Both the Roman Catholic, therefore, and the Buddhist may admit many of the marvels attributed to the relics of each other's saints ; though, in denying that these marvels prove the accuracy of each other's religious doctrines, each should remember that the same is true of his own.

In illustration of the real power of the imagination, I may instance the Maori superstition of the Taboo. According to the Maories, anyone who touches a tabooed object will assuredly die, the tabooed object being a sort of " anti-talisman ". Professor FRAZER [1] says : " Cases have been known of Maories dying of sheer fright on learning that they had unwittingly eaten the remains of a chief's dinner or handled something that belonged to him," since such objects were, *ipso facto*, tabooed. He gives the following case on good authority : " A woman, having partaken of some fine peaches from a basket, was told that they had come from a tabooed place. Immediately the basket dropped from her hands and she cried out in agony that the *atua* or godhead of the chief, whose divinity had been thus profaned, would kill her. That happened in the afternoon, and next day by twelve o'clock she was dead." For us the power of the taboo does not exist ; for the Maori, who implicitly believes in it, it is a very potent reality, but this power of the taboo resides not in external objects but in his own mind.

Dr HADDON [2] quotes a similar but still more remarkable story of a young Congo negro which very strikingly shows the power of the imagination. The young negro, " being on a journey, lodged at a friend's house ; the latter got a wild hen for his breakfast, and the young man asked if it were a wild hen. His host answered ' No.' Then he fell on heartily, and afterwards proceeded on his journey. After four years these two met together again, and his old friend asked him ' if he would eat a wild hen,' to which he answered that it was tabooed to

[1] Professor J. G. FRAZER, D.C.L. : *Psyche's Task* (1909), p. 7.
[2] ALFRED C. HADDON, Sc.D., F.R.S. : *Magic and Fetishism* (1906), p. 56.

him. Hereat the host began immediately to laugh, inquiring of him, ' What made him refuse it now, when he had eaten one at his table about four years ago ? ' At the hearing of this the negro immediately fell a-trembling, and suffered himself to be so far possessed with the effects of imagination that he died in less than twenty-four hours after."

There are, of course, many stories about amulets, *etc.*, which cannot be thus explained. For example, ELIHU RICH gives the following :—

" In 1568, we are told (Transl. of Salverte, p. 196) that the Prince of Orange condemned a Spanish prisoner to be shot at Juliers. The soldiers tied him to a tree and fired, but he was invulnerable. They then stripped him to see what armour he wore, but they found only an amulet bearing the figure of a lamb (the *Agnus Dei*, we presume). This was taken from him, and he was then killed by the first shot. De Baros relates that the Portuguese in like manner vainly attempted to destroy a Malay, so long as he wore a bracelet containing a bone set in gold, which rendered him proof against their swords. A similar marvel is related in the travels of the veracious Marco Polo. ' In an attempt of Kublai Khan to make a conquest of the island of Zipangu, a jealousy arose between the two commanders of the expedition, which led to an order for putting the whole garrison to the sword. In obedience to this order, the heads of all were cut off excepting of eight persons, who by the efficacy of a diabolical charm, consisting of a jewel or amulet introduced into the right arm, between the skin and the flesh, were rendered secure from the effects of iron, either to kill or wound. Upon this discovery being made, they were beaten with a heavy wooden club, and presently died.' " [1] I think, however, that these, and many similar stories, must be taken *cum grano salis*.

In conclusion, mention must be made of a very interesting and suggestive philosophical doctrine—the Law of Correspondences,—due in its explicit form to the Swedish philosopher, who was both scientist and mystic, EMANUEL SWEDENBORG. To deal in any way adequately with this important topic is totally impossible within the confines of the present discussion.[2] But, to put the matter as briefly as possible, it may be said that SWEDENBORG maintains (and the conclusion, I think, is valid) that all causation is from the spiritual world, physical causation being but secondary, or apparent—that is to say, a mere reflection, as it were, of the true process. He argues from this, thereby supplying a philosophical basis for the unanimous belief of the nature-mystics, that every natural object is the symbol (because the creation) of an idea or spiritual verity in its widest sense. Thus, there are symbols which are inherent in the nature of things, and symbols which are not. The former are genuine, the latter merely artificial. Writing from the transcendental point of view, ÉLIPHAS LÉVI says : " Ceremonies, vestments, perfumes, characters and figures being . . . necessary to enlist the imagination in the education of the will, the success of magical works depends upon the faithful observance of all the rites, which are in no sense

[1] ELIHU RICH : *The Occult Sciences,* p. 346.
[2] I may refer the reader to my *A Mathematical Theory of Spirit* (1912), chap. i., for a more adequate statement.

fantastic or arbitrary, having been transmitted to us by antiquity, and permanently subsisting by the essential laws of analogical realisation and of the correspondence which inevitably connects ideas and forms." [1] Some scepticism, perhaps, may be permitted as to the validity of the latter part of this statement, and the former may be qualified by the proviso that such things are only of value in the right education of the will, if they are, indeed, genuine, and not merely artificial, symbols. But the writer, as I think will be admitted, has grasped the essential point, and, to conclude our excursion, as we began it, with a definition, I will say that *the power of the talisman is the power of the mind (or imagination) brought into activity by means of a suitable symbol.*

[1] ÉLIPHAS LÉVI: *Transcendental Magic: its Doctrine and Ritual* (trans. by A. E. WAITE, 1896), p. 234.

VII

CEREMONIAL MAGIC IN THEORY AND PRACTICE

THE word " magic," if one may be permitted to say so, is itself almost magical—magical in its power to conjure up visions in the human mind. For some these are of bloody rites, pacts with the powers of darkness, and the lascivious orgies of the Saturnalia or Witches' Sabbath ; in other minds it has pleasanter associations, serving to transport them from the world of fact to the fairyland of fancy, where the purse of FORTUNATUS, the lamp and ring of ALADDIN, fairies, gnomes, jinn, and innumerable other strange beings flit across the scene in a marvellous kaleidoscope of ever-changing wonders. To the study of the magical beliefs of the past cannot be denied the interest and fascination which the marvellous and wonderful ever has for so many minds, many of whom, perhaps, cannot resist the temptation of thinking that there may be some element of truth in these wonderful stories. But the study has a greater claim to our attention ; for, as I have intimated already, magic represents a phase in the development of human thought, and the magic of the past was the womb from which sprang the science of the present, unlike its parent though it be.

What then is magic ? According to the dictionary definition—and this will serve us for the present—it is the (pretended) art of producing marvellous results by the aid of spiritual beings or arcane spiritual forces. Magic, therefore, is the practical complement of animism. Wherever man has really believed in the existence of a spiritual world, there do we find attempts to enter into communication with that world's inhabitants and to utilise its forces. Professor LEUBA[1] and others distinguish between propitiative behaviour towards the beings of the spiritual world, as marking the religious attitude, and coercive behaviour towards these beings as characteristic of the magical attitude ; but one form of behaviour merges by insensible degrees into the other, and the distinction (though a useful one) may, for our present purpose, be neglected.

Animism, " the Conception of Spirit everywhere " as Mr EDWARD CLODD [2] neatly calls it, and perhaps man's earliest view of natural phenomena, persisted in a modified form, as I have pointed out in " Some Characteristics of Mediæval Thought," throughout the Middle Ages. A belief in magic persisted likewise. In the writings of the Greek philosophers of the Neo-Platonic school, in that curious body of esoteric Jewish lore known as the Kabala, and in the works of later occult philosophers such as AGRIPPA

[1] JAMES H. LEUBA: *The Psychological Origin and the Nature of Religion* (1909), chap. ii.

[2] EDWARD CLODD: *Animism the Seed of Religion* (1905), p. 26.

and PARACELSUS, we find magic, or rather the theory upon which magic as an art was based, presented in its most philosophical form. If there is anything of value for modern thought in the theory of magic, here is it to be found ; and it is, I think, indeed to be found, absurd and fantastic though the practices based upon this philosophy, or which this philosophy was thought to substantiate, most certainly are. I shall here endeavour to give a sketch of certain of the outstanding doctrines of magical philosophy, some details concerning the art of magic, more especially as practised in the Middle Ages in Europe, and, finally, an attempt to extract from the former what I consider to be of real worth. We have already wandered down many of the byways of magical belief, and, indeed, the word " magic " may be made to cover almost every superstition of the past. To what we have already gained on previous excursions the present, I hope, will add what we need in order to take a synthetic view of the whole subject.

In the first place, something must be said concerning what is called the Doctrine of Emanations, a theory of prime importance in Neo-Platonic and Kabalistic ontology. According to this theory, everything in the universe owes its existence and virtue to an emanation from God, which divine emanation is supposed to descend, step by step (so to speak), through the hierarchies of angels and the stars, down to the things of earth, that which is nearer to the Source containing more of the divine nature than that which is relatively distant. As CORNELIUS AGRIPPA expresses it : " For God, in the first place is the end and beginning of all Virtues ; he gives the seal of the

Ideas to his servants, the Intelligences ; who as
faithful officers, sign all things intrusted to them
with an Ideal Virtue ; the Heavens and Stars, as
instruments, disposing the matter in the mean while
for the receiving of those forms which reside in
Divine Majesty (as saith Plato in Timeus) and to
be conveyed by Stars ; and the Giver of Forms
distributes them by the ministry of his Intelligences,
which he hath sct as Rulers and Controllers over his
Works, to whom such a power is intrusted to things
committed to them that so all Virtues of Stones,
Herbs, Metals, and all other things may come from
the Intelligences, the Governors.   The Form, therefore, and Virtue of things comes first from the *Ideas*,
then from the ruling and governing Intelligences,
then from the aspects of the Heavens disposing, and
lastly from the tempers of the Elements disposed,
answering the influences of the Heavens, by which
the Elements themselves are ordered, or disposed.
These kinds of operations, therefore, are performed
in these inferior things by express forms, and in the
Heavens by disposing virtues, in Intelligences by
mediating rules, in the Original Cause by *Ideas* and
exemplary forms, all which must of necessity agree
in the execution of the effect and virtue of every
thing.

" There is, therefore, a wonderful virtue and operation in every Herb and Stone, but greater in a Star,
beyond which, even from the governing Intelligences
everything receiveth and obtains many things for
itself, especially from the Supreme Cause, with whom
all things do mutually and exactly correspond, agreeing in an harmonious consent, as it were in hymns

always praising the highest Maker of all things. . . . There is, therefore, no other cause of the necessity of effects than the connection of all things with the First Cause, and their correspondency with those Divine patterns and eternal *Ideas* whence every thing hath its determinate and particular place in the exemplary world, from whence it lives and receives its original being : And every virtue of herbs, stones, metals, animals, words and speeches, and all things that are of God, is placed there." [1] As compared with the *ex nihilo* creationism of orthodox theology, this theory is as light is to darkness. Of course, there is much in CORNELIUS AGRIPPA's statement of it which is inacceptable to modern thought ; but these are matters of form merely, and do not affect the doctrine fundamentally. For instance, as a nexus between spirit and matter AGRIPPA places the stars : modern thought prefers the ether. The theory of emanations may be, and was, as a matter of fact, made the justification of superstitious practices of the grossest absurdity, but on the other hand it may be made the basis of a lofty system of transcendental philosophy, as, for instance, that of EMANUEL SWEDENBORG, whose ontology resembles in some respects that of the Neo-Platonists. AGRIPPA uses the theory to explain all the marvels which his age accredited, marvels which we know had for the most part no existence outside of man's imagination. I suggest, on the contrary, that the theory is really needed to explain the commonplace, since, in the last analysis, every bit of experience, every pheno-

[1] H. C. AGRIPPA: *Occult Philosophy*, bk. i., chap. xiii. (WHITEHEAD's edition, pp. 67–68).

menon, be it ever so ordinary—indeed the very fact
of experience itself,—is most truly marvellous and
magical, explicable only in terms of spirit. As
ÉLIPHAS LÉVI well says in one of his flashes of insight : " The supernatural is only the natural in an
extraordinary grade, or it is the exalted natural ; a
miracle is a phenomenon which strikes the multitude because it is unexpected ; the astonishing is
that which astonishes ; miracles are effects which
surprise those who are ignorant of their causes, or
assign them causes which are not in proportion to
such effects." [1]   But I am anticipating the sequel.

The doctrine of emanations makes the universe
one vast harmonious whole, between whose various
parts there is an exact analogy, correspondence, or
sympathetic relation. " Nature (the productive principle)," says IAMBLICHOS (3rd–4th century), the
Neo-Platonist, " in her peculiar way, makes a likeness of invisible principles through symbols in
visible forms." [2]   The belief that seemingly similar
things sympathetically affect one another, and that a
similar relation holds good between different things
which have been intimately connected with one
another as parts within a whole, is a very ancient
one. Most primitive peoples are very careful to
destroy all their nail-cuttings and hair-clippings,
since they believe that a witch gaining possession
of these might work them harm. For a similar
reason they refuse to reveal their *real* names, which

---

[1] ÉLIPHAS LÉVI : *Transcendental Magic, its Doctrine and
Ritual* (trans. by A. E. WAITE, 1896), p. 192.

[2] IAMBLICHOS : *Theurgia, or the Egyptian Mysteries* (trans.
by Dr ALEX. WILDER, New York, 1911), p. 239.

they regard as part of themselves, and adopt nick-
names for common use. The belief that a witch
can torment an enemy by making an image of his
person in clay or wax, correctly naming it, and
mutilating it with pins, or, in the case of a waxen
image, melting it by fire, is a very ancient one, and
was held throughout and beyond the Middle Ages.
The Sympathetic Powder of Sir KENELM DIGBY we
have already noticed, as well as other instances of
the belief in " sympathy," and examples of similar
superstitions might be multiplied almost indefinitely.
Such are generally grouped under the term " sympathetic magic " ; but inasmuch as all magical practices
assume that by acting on part of a thing, or a symbolic
representation of it, one acts magically on the whole,
or on the thing symbolised, the expression may in
its broadest sense be said to involve the whole of
magic.

The names of the Divine Being, angels and devils,
the planets of the solar system (including sun and
moon) and the days of the week, birds and beasts,
colours, herbs, and precious stones—all, according
to old-time occult philosophy, are connected by the
sympathetic relation believed to run through all
creation, the knowledge of which was essential to
the magician ; as well, also, the chief portions of the
human body, for man, as we have seen, was believed
to be a microcosm—a universe in miniature.   I have
dealt with this matter and exhibited some of the supposed correspondences in " The Belief in Talismans ".
Some further particulars are shown in the annexed
table, for which I am mainly indebted to AGRIPPA.
But, as in the case of the zodiacal gems already dealt

with, the old authorities by no means agree as to the majority of the planetary correspondences.

TABLE OF OCCULT CORRESPONDENCES

Arch-angel.	Angel.	Planet.	Part of Human Body.	Ani-mal.	Bird.	Precious Stone.
Raphael	Michael	Sun	Heart	Lion	Swan	Carbuncle
Gabriel	Gabriel	Moon	Left foot	Cat	Owl	Crystal
Camael	Zamael	Mars	Right hand	Wolf	Vulture	Diamond
Michael	Raphael	Mercury	Left hand	Ape	Stork	Agate
Zadikel	Sachiel	Jupiter	Head	Hart	Eagle	Sapphire (=Lapis lazuli)
Haniel	Anael	Venus	Generative organs	Goat	Dove	Emerald
Zaphkiel	Cassiel	Saturn	Right foot	Mole	Hoopoe	Onyx

The names of the angels are from Mr Mather's translation of *Clavicula Salomonis*; the other correspondences are from the second book of Agrippa's *Occult Philosophy*, chap. x.

In many cases these supposed correspondences are based, as will be obvious to the reader, upon purely trivial resemblances, and, in any case, whatever may be said—and I think a great deal may be said—in favour of the theory of symbology, there is little that may be adduced to support the old occultists' application of it.

So essential a part does the use of symbols play in all magical operations that we may, I think, modify the definition of " magic " adopted at the outset, and define " magic " as " an attempt to employ the powers of the spiritual world for the production of marvellous results, *by the aid of symbols.*" It has, on the other hand, been questioned whether the appeal to the spirit-world is an essential element in magic. But a close examination of magical practices always reveals at the root a belief in spiritual powers as the operating causes. The belief in talismans at first sight seems to have little to do with that in a supernatural realm ; but, as we have seen, the talisman was always a silent invocation of the powers of some spiritual being with which it was symbolically connected, and whose sign was engraved thereon. And, as Dr T. WITTON DAVIES well remarks with regard to " sympathetic magic " : " Even this could not, at the start, be anything other than a symbolic prayer to the spirit or spirits having authority in these matters. In so far as no spirit is thought of, it is a mere survival, and not magic at all. . . ." [1]

What I regard as the two essentials of magical practices, namely, the use of symbols and the appeal to the supernatural realm, are most obvious in what is called " ceremonial magic ". Mediæval ceremonial magic was subdivided into three chief branches—White Magic, Black Magic, and Necromancy. White magic was concerned with the evocations of angels, spiritual beings supposed to be essentially superior to mankind, concerning which I shall give some further details later—and the spirits of the elements,—which were, as I have mentioned in " Some Characteristics of Mediæval Thought," personifications of the primeval forces of Nature. As there were supposed to be four elements, fire, air, water, and earth, so there were supposed to be four classes of elementals or spirits of the elements, namely,

[1] Dr T. WITTON DAVIES: *Magic, Divination, and Demonology among the Hebrews and their Neighbours* (1898), p. 17.

Salamanders, Sylphs, Undines, and Gnomes, inhabiting these elements respectively, and deriving their characters therefrom. Concerning these curious beings, the inquisitive reader may gain some information from a quaint little book, by the Abbé de MONTFAUCON DE VILLARS, entitled *The Count of Gabalis, or Conferences about Secret Sciences* (1670), translated into English and published in 1680, which has recently been reprinted. The elementals, we learn therefrom, were, unlike other supernatural beings, thought to be mortal. They could, however, be rendered immortal by means of sexual intercourse with men or women, as the case might be ; and it was, we are told, to the noble end of endowing them with this great gift, that the sages devoted themselves.

Goëty, or black magic, was concerned with the evocation of demons and devils—spirits supposed to be superior to man in certain powers, but utterly depraved. Sorcery may be distinguished from witchcraft, inasmuch as the sorcerer attempted to command evil spirits by the aid of charms, *etc.*, whereas the witch or wizard was supposed to have made a pact with the Evil One ; though both terms have been rather loosely used, " sorcery " being sometimes employed as a synonym for " necromancy ". Necromancy was concerned with the evocation of the spirits of the dead : etymologically, the term stands for the art of foretelling events by means of such evocations, though it is frequently employed in the wider sense.

It would be unnecessary and tedious to give any detailed account of the methods employed in these magical arts beyond some general remarks. Mr A. E. WAITE gives full particulars of the various rituals in his *Book of Ceremonial Magic* (1911), to which the curious reader may be referred. The following will, in brief terms, convey a general idea of a magical evocation :—

Choosing a time when there is a favourable conjunction of the planets, the magician, armed with the implements of magical art, after much prayer and fasting, betakes himself to a suitable spot, alone, or perhaps accompanied by two trusty companions. All the articles he intends to employ, the vestments, the magic sword and lamp, the talismans, the book of spirits, *etc.*, have been specially prepared and consecrated. If he is about to invoke a martial spirit, the magician's vestment will be of a red colour, the talismans in virtue of which he may have power over the spirit will be of iron, the day chosen a Tuesday, and the incense and perfumes employed of a nature analogous to Mars. In a similar manner all the articles employed and the rites performed must in some way be symbolical of the spirit with which converse is desired. Having arrived at the spot, the magician first of all traces the magic circle within which, we are told, no evil spirit can enter ; he then commences the magic rite, involving various prayers and conjurations, a medley of meaningless words, and, in the case of the black art, a sacrifice. The spirit summoned then appears (at least, so we are told), and, after granting the magician's request, is licensed to depart—a matter, we are admonished, of great importance.

The question naturally arises, What were the

7

results obtained by these magical arts ? How far, if at all, was the magician rewarded by the attainment of his desires ? We have asked a similar question regarding the belief in talismans, and the reply which we there gained undoubtedly applies in the present case as well. Modern psychical research, as I have already pointed out, is supplying us with further evidence for the survival of human personality after bodily death than the innate conviction humanity in general seems to have in this belief, and the many reasons which idealistic philosophy advances in favour of it. The question of the reality of the phenomenon of " materialisation," that is, the bodily appearance of a discarnate spirit, such as is vouched for by spiritists, and which is what, it appears, was aimed at in necromancy (though why the discarnate should be better informed as to the future than the incarnate, I cannot suppose), must be regarded as *sub judice*.[1] Many cases of fraud in connection with the alleged production of this phenomenon have been detected in recent times ; but, inasmuch as the last word has not yet been said on the subject, we must allow the possibility that necromancy in the past may have been sometimes successful. But as to the existence of the angels and devils of magical belief—as well, one might add, of those of orthodox faith,—nothing can be adduced in evidence of this either from the results of psychical research or on *a priori* grounds.

Pseudo-DIONYSIUS classified the angels into three

[1] The late Sir WILLIAM CROOKES' *Experimental Researches in the Phenomena of Spiritualism* contains evidence in favour of the reality of this phenomenon very difficult to gainsay.

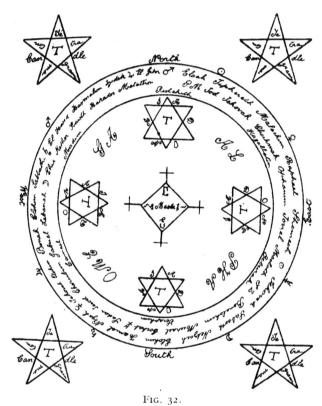

FIG. 32.

Magical Circle, from *The Lesser Key of Solomon the King.*

hierarchies, each subdivided into three orders, as under :—

> *First Hierarchy.* — Seraphim, Cherubim, and
> Thrones ;
> *Second Hierarchy.* — Dominions, Powers, and
> Authorities (or Virtues) ;
> *Third Hierarchy.*—Principalities, Archangels, and
> Angels,—

and this classification was adopted by AGRIPPA and others. Pseudo-DIONYSIUS explains the names of these orders as follows : " . . . the holy designation of the Seraphim denotes either that they are kindling or burning ; and that of the Cherubim, a fulness of knowledge or stream of wisdom. . . . The appellation of the most exalted and pre-eminent Thrones denotes their manifest exaltation above every grovelling inferiority, and their super-mundane tendency towards higher things ; . . . and their invariable and firmly-fixed settlement around the veritable Highest, with the whole force of their powers. . . . The explanatory name of the Holy Lordships [Dominions] denotes a certain unslavish elevation . . . superior to every kind of cringing slavery, indomitable to every subserviency, and elevated above every dissimularity, ever aspiring to the true Lordship and source of Lordship. . . . The appellation of the Holy Powers denotes a certain courageous and unflinching virility . . . vigorously conducted to the Divine imitation, not forsaking the Godlike movement through its own unmanliness, but unflinchingly looking to the super-essential and powerful-making power, and becoming a powerlike image of this, as

far as is attainable. . . . The appellation of the
Holy Authorities . . . denotes the beautiful and un-
confused good order, with regard to Divine receptions,
and the discipline of the super-mundane and intellectual authority . . . conducted indomitably, with
good order towards Divine things. . . . [And the
appellation] of the Heavenly Principalities manifests
their princely and leading function, after the Divine
example. . . ." [1] There is a certain grandeur in
these views, and if we may be permitted to understand by the orders of the hierarchy, " discrete "
degrees (to use SWEDENBORG'S term) of spiritual
reality — stages in spiritual involution,— we may
see in them a certain truth as well. As I said, all
virtue, power, and knowledge which man has from
God was believed to descend to him by way of these
angelical hierarchies, step by step ; and thus it was
thought that those of the lowest hierarchy alone were
sent from heaven to man. It was such beings that
white magic pretended to evoke. But the practical
occultists, when they did not make them altogether
fatuous, attributed to these angels characters not
distinguishable from those of the devils. The
description of the angels in the *Heptameron, or
Magical Elements,*[2] falsely attributed to PETER DE

---

[1] *On the Heavenly Hierarchy.* See the Rev. JOHN PARKER'S
translation of *The Works of* DIONYSIUS *the Areopagite*, vol. ii.
(1889), pp. 24, 25, 31, 32, and 36.

[2] The book, which first saw the light three centuries after
its alleged author's death, was translated into English by
ROBERT TURNER, and published in 1655 in a volume containing
the spurious *Fourth Book of Occult Philosophy*, attributed to
CORNELIUS AGRIPPA, and other magical works. It is from
this edition that I quote.

ABANO (1250–1316), may be taken as fairly characteristic. Of MICHAEL and the other spirits of Sunday he writes : " Their nature is to procure Gold, Gemmes, Carbuncles, Riches ; to cause one to obtain favour and benevolence ; to dissolve the enmities of men ; to raise men to honors ; to carry or take away infirmities." Of GABRIEL and the other spirits of Monday, he says : " Their nature is to give silver ; to convey things from place to place ; to make horses swift, and to disclose the secrets of persons both present and future." Of SAMAEL and the other spirits of Tuesday he says : " Their nature is to cause wars, mortality, death and combustions ; and to give two thousand Souldiers at a time ; to bring death, infirmities or health," and so on for RAPHAEL, SACHIEL, ANAEL, CASSIEL, and their colleagues.[1]

Concerning the evil planetary spirits, the spurious *Fourth Book of Occult Philosophy*, attributed to CORNELIUS AGRIPPA, informs us that the spirits of Saturn " appear for the most part with a tall, lean, and slender body, with an angry countenance, having four faces ; one in the hinder part of the head, one on the former part of the head, and on each side nosed or beaked : there likewise appeareth a face on each knee, of a black shining colour : their motion is the moving of the winde, with a kinde of earthquake : their signe is white earth, whiter than any Snow." The writer adds that their " particular forms are,—

A King having a beard, riding on a Dragon.

An Old man with a beard.

[1] *Op. cit.*, pp. 90, 92, and 94.

An Old woman leaning on a staffe.

A Hog.

A Dragon.

An Owl.

A black Garment.

A Hooke or Sickle.

A Juniper-tree."

Concerning the spirits of Jupiter, he says that they " appear with a body sanguine and cholerick, of a middle stature, with a horrible fearful motion ; but with a milde countenance, a gentle speech, and of the colour of Iron. The motion of them is flashings of Lightning and Thunder ; their signe is, there will appear men about the circle, who shall seem to be devoured of Lions," their particular forms being—

" A King with a Sword drawn, riding on a Stag.

A Man wearing a Mitre in long rayment.

A Maid with a Laurel-Crown adorned with Flowers.

A Bull.

A Stag.

A Peacock.

An azure Garment.

A Sword.

A Box-tree."

As to the Martian spirits, we learn that " they appear in a tall body, cholerick, a filthy countenance, of colour brown, swarthy or red, having horns like Harts horns, and Griphins claws, bellowing like wilde Bulls. Their Motion is like fire burning ; their signe Thunder and Lightning about the Circle. Their particular shapes are,—

A King armed riding upon a Wolf.

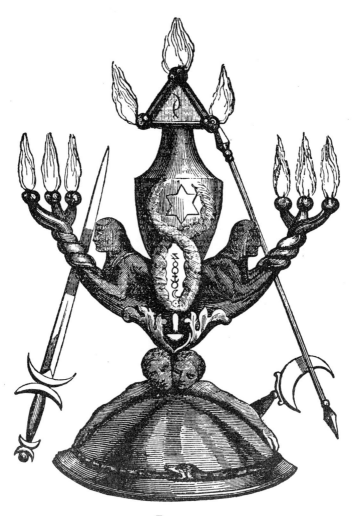

FIG. 33.
Magical Instruments—Lamp, Rod, Sword, and Dagger—according to
ÉLIPHAS LÉVI.

A Man armed.

A Woman holding a buckler on her thigh.

A Hee-goat.

A Horse.

A Stag.

A red Garment.

Wool.

A Cheeslip." [1]

The rest are described in equally fantastic terms.

I do not think I shall be accused of being unduly sceptical if I say that such beings as these could not have been evoked by any magical rites, because such beings do not and did not exist, save in the magician's own imagination. The proviso, however, is important, for, inasmuch as these fantastic beings did exist in the imagination of the credulous, therein they may, indeed, have been evoked. The whole of magic ritual was well devised to produce hallucination. A firm faith in the ritual employed, and a strong effort of will to bring about the desired result, were usually insisted upon as essential to the success of the operation.[2] A period of fasting prior to the experiment was also frequently prescribed as neces-

---

[1] *Op. cit.*, pp. 43–45.

[2] " MAGICAL AXIOM. In the circle of its action, every word creates that which it affirms.

" DIRECT CONSEQUENCE. He who affirms the devil, creates or makes the devil.

" *Conditions of Success in Infernal Evocations.* 1, Invincible obstinacy ; 2, a conscience at once hardened to crime and most subject to remorse and fear; 3, affected or natural ignorance ; 4, blind faith in all that is incredible ; 5, a completely false idea of God." (ÉLIPHAS LÉVI : *Op. cit.*, pp. 297 and 298.)

sary, which, by weakening the body, must have been conducive to hallucination. Furthermore, abstention from the gratification of the sexual appetite was stipulated in certain cases, and this, no doubt, had a similar effect, especially as concerns magical evocations directed to the satisfaction of the sexual impulse. Add to these factors the details of the ritual itself, the nocturnal conditions under which it was carried out, and particularly the suffumigations employed, which, most frequently, were of a narcotic nature, and it is not difficult to believe that almost any type of hallucination may have occurred. Such, as we have seen, was ÉLIPHAS LÉVI'S view of ceremonial magic ; and whatever may be said as concerns his own experiment therein (for one would have thought that the essential element of faith was lacking in this case), it is undoubtedly the true view as concerns the ceremonial magic of the past. As this author well says : " Witchcraft, properly so-called, that is ceremonial operation with intent to bewitch, acts only on the operator, and serves to fix and confirm his will, by formulating it with persistence and labour, the two conditions which make volition efficacious." [1]

EMANUEL SWEDENBORG in one place writes : " Magic is nothing but the perversion of order ; it is especially the abuse of correspondences." [2] A study of the ceremonial magic of the Middle Ages and the following century or two certainly justifies SWEDENBORG in writing of magic as something evil. The distinction, rigid enough in theory, between white and black, legitimate and illegitimate, magic, was,

[1] ÉLIPHAS LÉVI: *Op. cit.*, pp. 130 and 131.
[2] EMANUEL SWEDENBORG : *Arcana Cœlestia,* § 6692.

as I have indicated, extremely indefinite in practice. As Mr A. E. WAITE justly remarks: "Much that passed current in the west as White (*i.e.* permissible) Magic was only a disguised goeticism, and many of the resplendent angels invoked with divine rites reveal their cloven hoofs. It is not too much to say that a large majority of past psychological experiments were conducted to establish communication with demons, and that for unlawful purposes. The popular conceptions concerning the diabolical spheres, which have been all accredited by magic, may have been gross exaggerations of fact concerning rudimentary and perverse intelligences, but the wilful viciousness of the communicants is substantially untouched thereby."[1]

These "psychological experiments" were not, save, perhaps, in rare cases, carried out in the spirit of modern psychical research, with the high aim of the man of science. It was, indeed, far otherwise ; selfish motives were at the root of most of them ; and, apart from what may be termed "medicinal magic," it was for the satisfaction of greed, lust, revenge, that men and women had recourse to magical arts. The history of goëticism and witchcraft is one of the most horrible of all histories. The "Grimoires," witnesses to the superstitious folly of the past, are full of disgusting, absurd, and even criminal rites for the satisfaction of unlawful desires and passions. The Church was certainly justified in attempting to put down the practice of magic, but the means adopted in this design and the results to

[1] ARTHUR EDWARD WAITE: *The Occult Sciences* (1891), p. 51.

which they led were even more abominable than witchcraft itself. The methods of detecting witches and the tortures to which suspected persons were subjected to force them to confess to imaginary crimes, employed in so-called civilised England and Scotland and also in America, to say nothing of countries in which the " Holy " Inquisition held undisputed sway, are almost too horrible to describe. For details the reader may be referred to Sir WALTER SCOTT's *Letters on Demonology and Witchcraft* (1830), and (as concerns America) COTTON MATHER's *The Wonders of the Invisible World* (1692). The credulous Church and the credulous people were terribly afraid of the power of witchcraft, and, as always, fear destroyed their mental balance and made them totally disregard the demands of justice. The result may be well illustrated by what almost inevitably happens when a country goes to war ; for war, as the Hon. BERTRAND RUSSELL has well shown, is fear's offspring. Fear of the enemy causes the military party to persecute in an insensate manner, without the least regard to justice, all those of their fellow-men whom they consider are not heart and soul with them in their cause ; similarly the Church relentlessly persecuted its supposed enemies, of whom it was so afraid. No doubt some of the poor wretches that were tortured and killed on the charge of witchcraft really believed themselves to have made a pact with the devil, and were thus morally depraved, though, generally speaking, they were no more responsible for their actions than any other madmen. But the majority of the persons persecuted as witches and wizards were innocent even of this.

However, it would, I think, be unwise to disregard the existence of another side to the question of the validity and ethical value of magic, and to use the word only to stand for something essentially evil. SWEDENBORG, we may note, in the course of a long passage from the work from which I have already quoted, says that by " magic " is signified " the science of spiritual things ".[1] His position appears to be that there is a genuine magic, or science of spiritual things, and a false magic, that science perverted : a view of the matter which I propose here to adopt. The word " magic " itself is derived from the Greek " μαγος," the wise man of the East, and hence the strict etymological meaning of the term is " the wisdom or science of the magi "; and it is, I think, significant that we are told (and I see no reason to doubt the truth of it) that the magi were among the first to worship the new-born CHRIST.[2]

If there be an abuse of correspondences, or symbols, there surely must also be a use, to which the word " magic " is not inapplicable. As such, religious ritual, and especially the sacraments of the Christian Church, will, no doubt, occur to the minds of those who regard these symbols as efficacious, though they would probably hesitate to apply the term " magical " to them. But in using this term as applying thereto, I do not wish to suggest that any such rites or ceremonies possess, or can possess, any *causal* efficacy in the moral evolution of the soul. The will alone, in virtue of the power vouchsafed to it by the Source

[1] *Op. cit.*, § 5223.
[2] See *The Gospel according to* MATTHEW, chap. ii., verses 1 to 12.

of all power, can achieve this ; but I do think that
the soul may be assisted by ritual, harmoniously
related to the states of mind which it is desired to
induce. No doubt there is a danger of religious
ritual, especially when its meaning is lost, being
engaged in for its own sake. It is then mere superstition ;[1] and, in view of the danger of this degeneracy, many robust minds, such as the members
of the Society of Friends, prefer to dispense with
its aid altogether. When ritual is associated with
erroneous doctrines, the results are even more
disastrous, as I have indicated in " The Belief in
Talismans ". But when ritual is allied with, and
based upon, as adequately symbolising, the high
teaching of genuine religion, it may be, and, in fact,
is, found very helpful by many people. As such its
efficacy seems to me to be altogether magical, in the
best sense of that word.

But, indeed, I think a still wider application of
the word " magic " is possible. " All experience is
magic," says NOVALIS (1772–1801), " and only magically explicable " ;[2] and again : " It is only because of
the feebleness of our perceptions and activity that
we do not perceive ourselves to be in a fairy world."
No doubt it will be objected that the common experiences of daily life are " natural," whereas magic
postulates the " supernatural ". If, as is frequently
done, we use the term " natural," as relating exclus-

---

[1] As " ÉLIPHAS LÉVI " well says : " Superstition . . . is the
sign surviving the thought ; it is the dead body of a religious
rite." (*Op cit.*, p. 150.)

[2] NOVALIS : *Schriften* (ed. by LUDWIG TIECK and FR.
SCHLEGEL, 1805), vol. ii. p. 195.

ively to the physical realm, then, indeed, we may well speak of magic as " supernatural," because its aims are psychical. On the other hand, the term " natural " is sometimes employed as referring to the whole realm of order, and in this sense one can use the word " magic " as descriptive of Nature herself when viewed in the light of an idealistic philosophy, such as that of SWEDENBORG, in which all causation is seen to be essentially spiritual, the things of this world being envisaged as symbols of ideas or spiritual verities, and thus physical causation regarded as an appearance produced in virtue of the magical, non-causal efficacy of symbols.[1] Says CORNELIUS AGRIPPA : " . . . every day some natural thing is drawn by art and some divine thing is drawn by Nature which, the Egyptians, seeing, called Nature a Magicianess (*i.e.*) the very Magical power itself, in the attracting of like by like, and of suitable things by suitable." [2]

I would suggest, in conclusion, that there is nothing really opposed to the spirit of modern science in the thesis that " all experience is magic, and only magically explicable." Science does not pretend to reveal the fundamental or underlying cause of phenomena, does not pretend to answer the final Why ? This is rather the business of philosophy, though, in thus distinguishing between science and philosophy, I am far from insinuating that philosophy should be otherwise than scientific. We often hear religious but non-scientific men complain because scientific and perhaps equally as religious men do not in their

[1] For a discussion of the essentially magical character of inductive reasoning, see my *The Magic of Experience* (1915).

[2] *Op. cit.*, bk. i. chap. xxxvii. p. 119.

books ascribe the production of natural phenomena to the Divine Power. But if they were so to do they would be transcending their business as scientists. In every science certain simple facts of experience are taken for granted : it is the business of the scientist to reduce other and more complex facts of experience to terms of these data, not to explain these data themselves. Thus the physicist attempts to reduce other related phenomena of greater complexity to terms of simple force and motion ; but, What are force and motion ? Why does force produce or result in motion ? are questions which lie beyond the scope of physics. In order to answer these questions, if, indeed, this be possible, we must first inquire, How and why do these ideas of force and motion arise in our minds ? These problems land us in the psychical or spiritual world, and the term " magic " at once becomes significant.

" If," says THOMAS CARLYLE, " . . . we . . . have led thee into the true Land of Dreams ; and . . . thou lookest, even for moments, into the region of the Wonderful, and seest and feelest that thy daily life is girt with Wonder, and based on Wonder, and thy very blankets and breeches are Miracles,—then art thou profited beyond money's worth. . . ." [1]

[1] THOMAS CARLYLE : *Sartor Resartus,* bk. iii. chap. ix.

VIII

ARCHITECTURAL SYMBOLISM

I WAS once rash enough to suggest in an essay " On Symbolism in Art "[1] that " a true work of art is at once realistic, imaginative, and symbolical," and that its aim is to make manifest the spiritual significance of the natural objects dealt with. I trust that those artists (no doubt many) who disagree with me will forgive me—a man of science—for having ventured to express any opinion whatever on the subject. But, at any rate, if the suggestions in question are accepted, then a criterion for distinguishing between art and craft is at once available ; for we may say that, whilst craft aims at producing works which are physically useful, art aims at producing works which are spiritually useful. Architecture, from this point of view, is a combination of craft and art. It may, indeed, be said that the modern architecture which creates our dwelling-houses, factories, and even to a large extent our places of worship, is pure craft unmixed with art. On the other hand, it might be argued that such works of architecture are not always

[1] Published in *The Occult Review* for August 1912, vol. xvi. pp. 98 to 102.

devoid of decoration, and that "decorative art," even though the "decorative artist" is unconscious of this fact, is based upon rules and employs symbols which have a deep significance. The truly artistic element in architecture, however, is more clearly manifest if we turn our gaze to the past. One thinks at once, of course, of the pyramids and sphinx of Egypt, and the rich and varied symbolism of design and decoration of antique structures to be found in Persia and elsewhere in the East. It is highly probable that the Egyptian pyramids were employed for astronomical purposes, and thus subserved physical utility, but it seems no less likely that their shape was suggested by a belief in some system of geometrical symbolism, and was intended to embody certain of their philosophical or religious doctrines.

The mediæval cathedrals and churches of Europe admirably exhibit this combination of art with craft. Craft was needed to design and construct permanent buildings to protect worshippers from the inclemency of the weather ; art was employed not only to decorate such buildings, but it dictated to craft many points in connection with their design. The builders of the mediæval churches endeavoured so to construct their works that these might, as a whole and in their various parts, embody the truths, as they believed them, of the Christian religion : thus the cruciform shape of churches, their orientation, *etc.* The practical value of symbolism in church architecture is obvious. As Mr F. E. HULME remarks, "The sculptured fonts or stained-glass windows in the churches of the Middle Ages were full of teaching to a congregation of whom the greater

FIG. 34.
Agnus Dei, Sixteenth-century Font, Southfleet, Kent, from
COLLINS' *Symbolism of Animals.*
(*By kind permission of the Author.*)

FIG. 35.
Unicorn, Sixteenth-century Font, Southfleet, Kent, from
COLLINS' *Symbolism of Animals.*
(*By kind permission of the Author.*)

part could not read, to whom therefore one great avenue of knowledge was closed. The ignorant are especially impressed by pictorial teaching, and grasp its meaning far more readily than they can follow a written description or a spoken discourse." [1]

The subject of symbolism in church architecture is an extensive one, involving many side issues. In these excursions we shall consider only one aspect of it, namely, the symbolic use of animal forms in English church architecture.

As Mr COLLINS, who has written, in recent years, an interesting work on this topic of much use to archæologists as a book of data,[2] points out, the great sources of animal symbolism were the famous *Physiologus* and other natural history books of the Middle Ages (generally called " Bestiaries "), and the Bible, mystically understood. The modern tendency is somewhat unsympathetic towards any attempt to interpret the Bible symbolically, and certainly some of the interpretations that have been forced upon it in the name of symbolism are crude and fantastic enough. But in the belief of the mystics, culminating in the elaborate system of correspondences of SWEDENBORG, that every natural object, every event in the history of the human race, and every word of the Bible, has a symbolic and spiritual significance, there is, I think, a fundamental truth. We must, however, as I have suggested already, distinguish between true and forced symbol-

---

[1] F. EDWARD HULME, F.L.S., F.S.A. : *The History, Principles, and Practice of Symbolism in Christian Art* (1909), p. 2.

[2] ARTHUR H. COLLINS, M.A. : *Symbolism of Animals and Birds represented in English Church Architecture* (1913).

ism. The early Christians employed the fish as a symbol of Christ, because the Greek word for fish, ἰχθύς, is obtained by *notariqon* [1] from the phrase Ἰησοῦς Χριστός, θεοῦ Υἱός, Σωτήρ—" JESUS CHRIST, the Son of God, the Saviour." Of course, the obvious use of such a symbol was its entire unintelligibility to those who had not yet been instructed in the mysteries of the Christian faith, since in the days of persecution some degree of secrecy was necessary. But the symbol has significance only in the Greek language, and that of an entirely arbitrary nature. There is nothing in the nature of the fish, apart from its name in Greek, which renders it suitable to be used as a symbol of CHRIST. Contrast this pseudo-symbol, however, with that of the Good Shepherd, the Lamb of God (fig. 34), or the Lion of Judah. Here we have what may be regarded as true symbols, something of whose meanings are clear to the smallest degree of spiritual sight, even though the second of them has frequently been badly misinterpreted.

It was a belief in the spiritual or moral significance of nature similar to that of the mystical expositors of the Bible, that inspired the mediæval naturalists. The Bestiaries almost invariably conclude the account of each animal with the moral that might be drawn from its behaviour. The interpretations are frequently very far-fetched, and as the writers were more interested in the morals than in the facts of natural history themselves, the supposed facts from which they drew their morals were frequently very

[1] A Kabalistic process by which a word is formed by taking the initial letters of a sentence or phrase.

Fig. 37.

Twelfth-century South Door, Barfreston Church, Kent, showing Griffin and other Symbols, from COLLINS' *Symbolism of Animals.*

(*By kind permission of the Author.*)

Fig. 36.

Pelican in her Piety, inset in Pulpit, Aldington, Kent, from COLLINS' *Symbolism of Animals.*

far from being of the nature of facts. Sometimes the product of this inaccuracy is grotesque, as shown by the following quotation : " The elephants are in an absurd way typical of Adam and Eve, who ate of the forbidden fruit, and also have the dragon for their enemy. It was supposed that the elephant . . . used to sleep by leaning against a tree. The hunters would come by night, and cut the trunk through. Down he would come, roaring helplessly. None of his friends would be able to help him, until a small elephant should come and lever him up with his trunk. This small elephant was symbolic of Jesus Christ, Who came in great humility to rescue the human race which had fallen ' through a tree.' " [1]

In some cases, though the symbolism is based upon quite erroneous notions concerning natural history, and is so far fantastic, it is not devoid of charm. The use of the pelican to symbolise the Saviour is a case in point. Legend tells us that when other food is unobtainable, the pelican thrusts its bill into its breast (whence the red colour of the bill) and feeds its young with its life-blood. Were this only a fact, the symbol would be most appropriate. There is another and far less charming form of the legend, though more in accord with current perversions of Christian doctrine, according to which the pelican uses its blood to revive its young, after having slain them through anger aroused by the great provocation which they are supposed to give it. For an example of the use of the pelican in church architecture see fig. 36.

Mention must also be made of the purely fabulous

[1] A. H. COLLINS : *Symbolism of Animals, etc.,* pp. 41 and 42.

animals of the Bestiaries, such as the basilisk, centaur, dragon, griffin, hydra, mantichora, unicorn, phœnix, *etc.* The centaur (fig. 39) was a beast, half man, half horse. It typified the flesh or carnal mind of man, and the legend of the perpetual war between the centaur and a certain tribe of simple savages who were said to live in trees in India, symbolised the combat between the flesh and the spirit.[1]

With bow and arrow in its hands the centaur forms the astrological sign Sagittarius (or the Archer). An interesting example of this sign occurring in church architecture is to be found on the western doorway of Portchester Church—a most beautiful piece of Norman architecture. " This sign of the Zodiac," writes the Rev. Canon VAUGHAN, M.A., a former Vicar of Portchester, " was the badge of King Stephen, and its presence on the west front [of Portchester Church] seems to indicate, what was often the case elsewhere, that the elaborate Norman carving was not carried out until after the completion of the building."[2] The facts, however, that this Sagittarius is accompanied on the other side of the door-way by a couple of fishes, which form the astrological sign Pisces (or the Fishes), and that these two signs are what are termed, in astrological phraseology, the " houses " of the planet Jupiter, the " Major Fortune," suggest that the architect responsible for the design, influenced by the astrological notions of his day, may have put the signs there in order to

[1] A. H. COLLINS: *Symbolism of Animals, etc.*, pp. 150 and 153.

[2] Rev. Canon VAUGHAN, M.A.: *A Short History of Portchester Castle*, p. 14.

Fig. 38.
Western Doorway of Porchester Church, Hants,
showing Sagittarius and Pisces.

attract Jupiter's beneficent influence. Or he may have had the Sagittarius carved for the reason Canon VAUGHAN suggests, and then, remembering how good a sign it was astrologically, had the Pisces added to complete the effect.[1]

The phœnix and griffin we have encountered already in our excursions. The latter, we are told, inhabits desert places in India, where it can find nothing for its young to eat. It flies away to other regions to seek food, and is sufficiently strong to carry off an ox. Thus it symbolises the devil, who is ever anxious to carry away our souls to the deserts of hell. Fig. 37 illustrates an example of the use of this symbolic beast in church architecture.

---

[1] Two other possible explanations of the Pisces have been suggested by the Rev. A. HEADLEY. In his MS. book written in 1888, when he was Vicar of Portchester, he writes: "I have discovered an interesting proof that it [the Church] was finished in Stephen's reign, namely, the figure of Sagittarius in the Western Doorway.

"Stephen adopted this as his badge for the double reason that it formed part of the arms of the city of Blois, and that the sun was in Sagittarius in December when he came to the throne. I, therefore, conclude that this badge was placed where it is to mark the completion of the church.

"There is another sign of the Zodiac in the archway, apparently Pisces. This may have been chosen to mark the month in which the church was finished, or simply on account of its nearness to the sea. At one time I fancied it might refer to March, the month in which Lady Day occurred, thus referring to the Patron Saint, St Mary. As the sun leaves Pisces just before Lady Day this does not explain it. Possibly in the old calendar it might do so. This is a matter for further research." (I have to thank the Rev. H. LAWRENCE FRY, present Vicar of Portchester, for this quotation, and the Rev. A. HEADLEY for permission to utilise it.)

The mantichora is described by PLINY (whose statements were unquestioningly accepted by the mediæval naturalists), on the authority of CTESIAS (*fl.* 400 B.C.), as having " A triple row of teeth, which fit into each other like those of a comb, the face and ears of a man, and azure eyes, is the colour of blood, has the body of the lion, and a tail ending in a sting, like that of the scorpion. Its voice resembles the union of the sound of the flute and the trumpet ; it is of excessive swiftness, and is particularly fond of human flesh." [1]

Concerning the unicorn, in an eighteenth-century work on natural history we read that this is " a Beast, which though doubted of by many Writers, yet is by others thus described : He has but one Horn, and that an exceedingly rich one, growing out of the middle of his Forehead. His Head resembles an Hart's, his Feet an Elephant's, his tail a Boar's, and the rest of his Body an Horse's. The Horn is about a Foot and half in length. His Voice is like the Lowing of an Ox. His Mane and Hair are of a yellowish Colour. His Horn is as hard as Iron, and as rough as any File, twisted or curled, like a flaming Sword ; very straight, sharp, and every where black, excepting the Point. Great Virtues are attributed to it, in expelling of Poison and curing of several Diseases. He is not a Beast of prey." [2] The method of capturing the animal believed in by mediæval writers was a curious one. The following is a literal

---

[1] PLINY : *Natural History*, bk. viii. chap. xxx. (BOSTOCK and RILEY's trans., vol. ii., 1855, p. 280.)

[2] [THOMAS BOREMAN]: *A Description of Three Hundred Animals* (1730), p. 6.

FIG. 39.

Centaur, from VLYSSIS ALDROVANDI'S *Monstrorum Historia* (1642).

FIG. 40.

Mantichora, from *A Description of Three Hundred Animals* (1730).

translation from the *Bestiary* of Philippe de Thaun
(12th century) :—

" Monosceros is an animal which has one horn on its head,
   Therefore it is so named ; it has the form of a goat,
   It is caught by means of a virgin, now hear in what manner.
   When a man intends to hunt it and to take and ensnare it
   He goes to the forest where is its repair ;
   There he places a virgin, with her breast uncovered,
   And by its smell the monosceros perceives it ;
   Then it comes to the virgin, and kisses her breast,
   Falls asleep on her lap, and so comes to its death ;
   The man arrives immediately, and kills it in its sleep,
   Or takes it alive and does as he likes with it.
   It signifies much, I will not omit to tell it you.

   " Monosceros is Greek, it means *one horn* in French :
   A beast of such a description signifies Jesus Christ ;
   One God he is and shall be, and was and will continue so ;
   He placed himself in the virgin, and took flesh for man's sake,
   And for virginity to show chastity ;
   To a virgin he *appeared* and a virgin conceived him,
   A virgin she is, and will be, and will remain always.
   Now hear briefly the signification.

   " This animal in truth signifies God ;
   Know that the virgin signifies St Mary ;
   By her breast we understand similarly Holy Church ;
   And then by the kiss it ought to signify,
   That a man when he sleeps is in semblance of death ;
   God slept as man, who suffered death on the cross,
   And his destruction was our redemption,
   And his labour our repose,
   Thus God deceived the Devil by a proper semblance ;
   Soul and body were one, so was God and man,
   And this is the signification of an animal of that description."[1]

---

[1] *Popular Treatises on Science written during the Middle
Ages in Anglo-Saxon, Anglo-Norman, and English,* ed. by
Thomas Wright (Historical Society of Science, 1841), pp. 81–82.

This being the current belief concerning the symbolism of the unicorn in the Middle Ages, it is not surprising to find this animal utilised in church architecture; for an example see fig. 35.

The belief in the existence of these fabulous beasts may very probably have been due to the materialising of what were originally nothing more than mere arbitrary symbols, as I have already suggested of the phœnix.[1] Thus the account of the mantichora may, as BOSTOCK has suggested, very well be a description of certain hieroglyphic figures, examples of which are still to be found in the ruins of Assyrian and Persian cities. This explanation seems, on the whole, more likely than the alternative hypothesis that such beliefs were due to mal-observation; though that, no doubt, helped in their formation.

It may be questioned, however, whether the architects and preachers of the Middle Ages altogether believed in the strange fables of the Bestiaries. As Mr COLLINS says in reply to this question: "Probably they were credulous enough. But, on the whole, we may say that the truth of the story was just what they did not trouble about, any more than some clergymen are particular about the absolute truth of the stories they tell children from the pulpit. The application, the lesson, is the thing!" With their desire to interpret Nature spiritually, we ought, I think, to sympathise. But there was one truth they had yet to learn, namely, that in order to interpret Nature spiritually, it is necessary first to understand her aright in her literal sense.

[1] " Superstitions concerning Birds."

IX

THE QUEST OF THE PHILOSOPHER'S STONE

THE need of unity is a primary need of human thought. Behind the varied multiplicity of the world of phenomena, primitive man, as I have indicated on a preceding excursion, begins to seek, more or less consciously, for that Unity which alone is Real. And this statement not only applies to the first dim gropings of the primitive human mind, but sums up almost the whole of science and philosophy; for almost all science and philosophy is explicitly or implicitly a search for unity, for one law or one love, one matter or one spirit. That which is the aim of the search may, indeed, be expressed under widely different terms, but it is always conceived to be the unity in which all multiplicity is resolved, whether it be thought of as one final law of necessity, which all things obey, and of which all the various other " laws of nature " are so many special and limited applications ; or as one final love for which all things are created, and to which all things aspire ; as one matter of which all bodies are but varying forms ; or as one spirit, which is the life of all things, and of which all things are so many manifestations. Every scientist and philosopher is a merchant seeking for goodly pearls, willing to sell every pearl that he has, if he may secure the One Pearl beyond price, because he knows that in that One Pearl all others are included.

This search for unity in multiplicity, however, is not confined to the acknowledged scientist and philosopher. More or less unconsciously everyone is engaged in this quest. Harmony and unity are the very fundamental laws of the human mind itself, and, in a sense, all mental activity is the endeavour to bring about a state of harmony and unity in the mind. No two ideas that are contradictory of one another, and are perceived to be of this nature, can permanently exist in any sane man's mind. It is true that many people try to keep certain portions of their mental life in water-tight compartments ; thus some try to keep their religious convictions and their business ideas, or their religious faith and their scientific knowledge, separate from another one—and, it seems, often succeed remarkably well in so doing. But, ultimately, the arbitrary mental walls they have erected will break down by the force of their own ideas. Contradictory ideas from different compartments will then present themselves to consciousness at the same moment of time, and the result of the perception of their contradictory nature will be mental anguish and turmoil, persisting until one set of ideas is conquered and overcome by the other, and harmony and unity are restored.

It is true of all of us, then, that we seek for Unity— unity in mind and life. Some seek it in science and a life of knowledge; some seek it in religion and a life of faith; some seek it in human love and find it in the life of service to their fellows; some seek it in pleasure and the gratification of the senses' demands; some seek it in the harmonious development of all the facets of their being. Many the methods, right and wrong; many the terms under which the One is conceived, true and false—in a sense, to use the phraseology of a bygone system of philosophy, we are all, consciously or unconsciously, following paths that lead thither or paths that lead away, seekers in the quest of the Philosopher's Stone.

Let us, in these excursions in the byways of thought, consider for a while the form that the quest of fundamental unity took in the hands of those curious mediæval philosophers, half mystics, half experimentalists in natural things—that are known by the name of " alchemists."

The common opinion concerning alchemy is that it was a pseudo-science or pseudo-art flourishing during the Dark Ages, and having for its aim the conversion of common metals into silver and gold by means of a most marvellous and wholly fabulous agent called the Philosopher's Stone, that its devotees were half knaves, half fools, whose views concerning Nature were entirely erroneous, and whose objects were entirely mercenary. This opinion is not absolutely destitute of truth; as a science alchemy involved many fantastic errors; and in the course of its history it certainly proved attractive to both knaves and fools. But if this opinion involves some element of truth, it involves a far greater proportion of error. Amongst the alchemists are numbered some of the

greatest intellects of the Middle Ages — ROGER
BACON (c. 1214–1294), for example, who might
almost be called the father of experimental science.
And whether or not the desire for material wealth
was a secondary object, the true aim of the genuine
alchemist was a much nobler one than this—as one
of them exclaims with true scientific fervour :
" Would to God . . . all men might become adepts
in our Art—for then gold, the great idol of mankind,
would lose its value, and we should prize it only for
its scientific teaching." [1]   Moreover, recent develop-
ments in physical and chemical science seem to indicate that the alchemists were not so utterly wrong in
their concept of Nature as has formerly been supposed
—that, whilst they certainly erred in both their
methods and their interpretations of individual
phenomena, they did intuitively grasp certain fundamental facts concerning the universe of the very
greatest importance.

Suppose, however, that the theories of the alchemists are entirely erroneous from beginning to
end, and are nowhere relieved by the merest glimmer
of truth.   Still they were believed to be true, and
this belief had an important influence upon human
thought.   Many men of science have, I am afraid,
been too prone to regard the mystical views of the
alchemists as unintelligible ; but, whatever their
theories may be to us, these theories were certainly
very real to them : it is preposterous to maintain
that the writings of the alchemists are without mean-

---

[1] EIRENÆUS PHILALETHES : *An Open Entrance to the Closed
Palace of the King.* (See *The Hermetic Museum, Restored and
Enlarged,* ed. by A. E. WAITE, 1893, vol. ii. p. 178.)

ing, even though their views are altogether false. And the more false their views are believed to be, the more necessary does it become to explain why they should have gained such universal credit. Here we have problems into which scientific inquiry is not only legitimate, but, I think, very desirable,— apart altogether from the question of the truth or falsity of alchemy as a science, or its utility as an art. What exactly was the system of beliefs grouped under the term " alchemy," and what was its aim ? Why were the beliefs held ?   What was their precise influence upon human thought and culture ?

It was in order to elucidate problems of this sort, as well as to determine what elements of truth, if any, there are in the theories of the alchemists, that The Alchemical Society was founded in 1912, mainly through my own efforts and those of my confrères, and for the first time someting like justice was being done to the memory of the alchemists when the Society's activities were stayed by that greatest calamity of history, the European War.

Some students of the writings of the alchemists have advanced a very curious and interesting theory as to the aims of the alchemists, which may be termed " the transcendental theory ". According to this theory, the alchemists were concerned only with the mystical processes affecting the soul of man, and their chemical references are only to be understood symbolically. In my opinion, however, this view of the subject is rendered untenable by the lives of the alchemists themselves ; for, as Mr WAITE has very fully pointed out in his *Lives of Alchemystical Philosophers* (1888), the lives of the alchemists show them to have been mainly concerned with chemical and physical processes ; and, indeed, to their labours we owe many valuable discoveries of a chemical nature. But the fact that such a theory should ever have been formulated, and should not be altogether lacking in consistency, may serve to direct our attention to the close connection between alchemy and mysticism.

If we wish to understand the origin and aims of alchemy we must endeavour to recreate the atmosphere of the Middle Ages, and to look at the subject from the point of view of the alchemists themselves. Now, this atmosphere was, as I have indicated in a previous essay, surcharged with mystical theology and mystical philosophy. Alchemy, so to speak, was generated and throve in a dim religious light. We cannot open a book by any one of the better sort of alchemists without noticing how closely their theology and their chemistry are interwoven, and what a remarkably religious view they take of their subject. Thus one alchemist writes: " In the first place, let every devout and God-fearing chemist and student of this Art consider that this arcanum should be regarded, not only as a truly great, but as a most holy Art (seeing that it typifies and shadows out the highest heavenly good). Therefore, if any man desire to reach this great and unspeakable Mystery, he must remember that it is obtained not by the might of man, but by the grace of God, and that not our will or desire, but only the mercy of the Most High, can bestow it upon us. For this reason you must first of all cleanse your heart, lift it up to Him alone, and ask of Him this gift in true, earnest and undoubting prayer. He alone can give and bestow it." [1] Whilst another alchemist declares : " I am firmly persuaded that any unbeliever who got truly to know this Art, would straightway confess the truth of our Blessed Religion, and believe in the Trinity and in our Lord JESUS CHRIST." [2]

Now, what I suggest is that the alchemists constructed their chemical theories for the main part by means of *a priori* reasoning, and that the premises from which they started were (i.) the truth of mystical theology, especially the doctrine of the soul's regeneration, and (ii.) the truth of mystical philosophy, which asserts that the objects of Nature are symbols of spiritual verities. There is, I think, abundant evidence to show that alchemy was a more or less deliberate attempt to apply, according to the principles of analogy, the doctrines of religious mysticism to chemical and physical phenomena. Some of this evidence I shall attempt to put forward in this essay.

In the first place, however, I propose to say a few words more in description of the theological and philosophical doctrines which so greatly influenced the alchemists, and which, I believe, they borrowed for their attempted explanations of chemical and physical phenomena. This system of doctrine I have termed " mysticism "—a word which is unfortunately equivocal, and has been used to denote various systems of religious and philosophical thought,

---

[1] *The Sophic Hydrolith ; or, Water Stone of the Wise.* (See *The Hermetic Museum*, vol. i. pp. 74 and 75.)

[2] PETER BONUS : *The New Pearl of Great Price* (trans. by A. E. WAITE, 1894), p. 275.

from the noblest to the most degraded. I have, therefore, further to define my usage of the term.

By mystical theology I mean that system of religious thought which emphasises the unity between Creator and creature, though not necessarily to the extent of becoming pantheistic. Man, mystical theology asserts, has sprung from God, but has fallen away from Him through self-love. Within man, however, is the seed of divine grace, whereby, if he will follow the narrow road of self-renunciation, he may be regenerated, born anew, becoming transformed into the likeness of God and ultimately indissolubly united to God in love. God is at once the Creator and the Restorer of man's soul, He is the Origin as well as the End of all existence ; and He is also the Way to that End. In Christian mysticism, CHRIST is the Pattern, towards which the mystic strives ; CHRIST also is the means towards the attainment of this end.

By mystical philosophy I mean that system of philosophical thought which emphasises the unity of the Cosmos, asserting that God and the spiritual may be perceived immanent in the things of this world, because all things natural are symbols and emblems of spiritual verities. As one of the *Golden Verses* attributed to PYTHAGORAS, which I have quoted in a previous essay, puts it : " The Nature of this Universe is in all things alike "; commenting upon which, HIEROCLES, writing in the fifth or sixth century, remarks that " Nature, in forming this Universe after the Divine Measure and Proportion, made it in all things conformable and like to itself, analogically in different manners. Of all the different species, diffused throughout the whole, it made, as it were, an Image of the Divine Beauty, imparting variously to the copy the perfections of the Original."[1] We have, however, already encountered so many instances of this belief, that no more need be said here concerning it.

In fine, as Dean INGE well says: " Religious Mysticism may be defined as the attempt to realise the presence of the living God in the soul and in nature, or, more generally, as *the attempt to realise, in thought and feeling, the immanence of the temporal in the eternal, and of the eternal in the temporal.*" [2]

Now, doctrines such as these were not only very prevalent during the Middle Ages, when alchemy so greatly flourished, but are of great antiquity, and were undoubtedly believed in by the learned class in Egypt and elsewhere in the East in those remote days when, as some think, alchemy originated, though the evidence, as will, I hope, become plain as we proceed, points to a later and post-Christian origin for the central theorem of alchemy. So far as we can judge from their writings, the more important alchemists were convinced of the truth of these doctrines, and it was with such beliefs in mind that they commenced their investigations of physical and chemical phenomena. Indeed, if we may judge by the esteem in which the Hermetic maxim, " What is above is as that which is below, what is below is as that which is above, to accomplish the miracles of

---

[1] *Commentary of* HIEROCLES *on the Golden Verses of* PYTHAGORAS (trans. by N. ROWE, 1906), pp. 101 and 102.

[2] WILLIAM RALPH INGE, M.A.: *Christian Mysticism* (the Bampton Lectures, 1899), p. 5.

the One Thing," was held by every alchemist, we are justified in asserting that the mystical theory of the spiritual significance of Nature—a theory with which, as we have seen, is closely connected the Neoplatonic and Kabalistic doctrine that all things emanate in series from the Divine Source of all Being—was at the very heart of alchemy. As writes one alchemist : " . . . the Sages have been taught of God that this natural world is only an image and material copy of a heavenly and spiritual pattern ; that the very existence of this world is based upon the reality of its celestial archetype ; and that God has created it in imitation of the spiritual and invisible universe, in order that men might be the better enabled to comprehend His heavenly teaching, and the wonders of His absolute and ineffable power and wisdom. Thus the sage sees heaven reflected in Nature as in a mirror ; and he pursues this Art, not for the sake of gold or silver, but for the love of the knowledge which it reveals ; he jealously conceals it from the sinner and the scornful, lest the mysteries of heaven should be laid bare to the vulgar gaze." [1]

The alchemists, I hold, convinced of the truth of this view of Nature, *i.e.* that principles true of one plane of being are true also of all other planes, adopted analogy as their guide in dealing with the facts of chemistry and physics known to them. They endeavoured to explain these facts by an application to them of the principles of mystical theology, their

[1] MICHAEL SENDIVOGIUS (?) : *The New Chemical Light, Pt. II., Concerning Sulphur.* (See *The Hermetic Museum,* vol. ii. p. 138.)

chief aim being to prove the truth of these principles
as applied to the facts of the natural realm, and by
studying natural phenomena to become instructed in
spiritual truth. They did not proceed by the sure,
but slow, method of modern science, *i.e.* the method
of induction, which questions experience at every
step in the construction of a theory ; but they boldly
allowed their imaginations to leap ahead and to
formulate a complete theory of the Cosmos on the
strength of but few facts. This led them into many
fantastic errors, but I would not venture to deny them
an intuitive perception of certain fundamental truths
concerning the constitution of the Cosmos, even if
they distorted these truths and dressed them in a
fantastic garb.

Now, as I hope to make plain in the course of
this excursion, the alchemists regarded the discovery
of the Philosopher's Stone and the transmutation of
" base " metals into gold as the consummation of
the proof of the doctrines of mystical theology as
applied to chemical phenomena, and it was as such
that they so ardently sought to achieve the *magnum
opus*, as this transmutation was called. Of course,
it would be useless to deny that many, accepting the
truth of the great alchemical theorem, sought for
the Philosopher's Stone because of what was claimed
for it in the way of material benefits. But, as I have
already indicated, with the nobler alchemists this
was not the case, and the desire for wealth, if present
at all, was merely a secondary object.

The idea expressed in DALTON's atomic hypothesis (1802), and universally held during the nineteenth century, that the material world is made up

of a certain limited number of elements unalterable in quantity, subject in themselves to no change or development, and inconvertible one into another, is quite alien to the views of the alchemists. The alchemists conceived the universe to be a unity; they believed that all material bodies had been developed from one seed; their elements are merely different forms of one matter and, therefore, convertible one into another. They were thoroughgoing evolutionists with regard to the things of the material world, and their theory concerning the evolution of the metals was, I believe, the direct outcome of a metallurgical application of the mystical doctrine of the soul's development and regeneration. The metals, they taught, all spring from the same seed in Nature's womb, but are not all equally matured and perfect; for, as they say, although Nature always intends to produce only gold, various impurities impede the process. In the metals the alchemists saw symbols of man in the various stages of his spiritual development. Gold, the most beautiful as well as the most untarnishable metal, keeping its beauty permanently, unaffected by sulphur, most acids, and fire—indeed, purified by such treatment,—gold, to the alchemist, was the symbol of regenerate man, and therefore he called it " a noble metal ". Silver was also termed " noble "; but it was regarded as less mature than gold, for, although it is undoubtedly beautiful and withstands the action of fire, it is corroded by nitric acid and is blackened by sulphur; it was, therefore, considered to be analogous to the regenerate man at a lower stage of his development. Possibly we shall not be far wrong in using SWEDENBORG's terms, " celestial " to describe the man of gold, " spiritual " to designate him of silver. Lead, on the other hand, the alchemists regarded as a very immature and impure metal: heavy and dull, corroded by sulphur and nitric acid, and converted into a calx by the action of fire,—lead, to the alchemists, was a symbol of man in a sinful and unregenerate condition.

The alchemists assumed the existence of three principles in the metals, their obvious reason for so doing being the mystical threefold division of man into body, soul (*i.e.* affections and will), and spirit (*i.e.* intelligence), though the principle corresponding to body was a comparatively late introduction in alchemical philosophy. This latter fact, however, is no argument against my thesis ; because, of course, I do not maintain that the alchemists started out with their chemical philosophy ready made, but gradually worked it out, by incorporating in it further doctrines drawn from mystical theology. The three principles just referred to were called " mercury," " sulphur," and " salt " ; and they must be distinguished from the common bodies so designated (though the alchemists themselves seem often guilty of confusing them). " Mercury " is the metallic principle *par excellence*, conferring on metals their brightness and fusibility, and corresponding to the spirit or intelligence in man.[1] " Sulphur," the principle of combustion and colour, is the analogue of the soul. Many alchemists postulated two sulphurs in the metals, an inward and an

[1] The identification of the god MERCURY with THOTH, the Egyptian god of learning, is worth noticing in this connection.

outward.[1]   The outward sulphur was thought to be
the chief cause of metallic impurity, and the reason
why all (known) metals, save gold and silver, were
acted on by fire.   The inward sulphur, on the other
hand, was regarded as essential to the development
of the metals : pure mercury, we are told, matured
by a pure inward sulphur yields pure gold.   Here
again it is evident that the alchemists borrowed
their theories from mystical theology ; for, clearly,
inward sulphur is nothing else than the equivalent
to love of God ; outward sulphur to love of self.
Intelligence (mercury) matured by love to God (inward sulphur) exactly expresses the spiritual state
of the regenerate man according to mystical theology.
There is no reason, other than their belief in analogy,
why the alchemists should have held such views
concerning the metals.   " Salt," the principle of
solidity and resistance to fire, corresponding to the
body in man, plays a comparatively unimportant
part in alchemical theory, as does its prototype in
mystical theology.

Now, as I have pointed out already, the central
theorem of mystical theology is, in Christian terminology, that of the regeneration of the soul by the
Spirit of CHRIST.   The corresponding process in
alchemy is that of the transmutation of the " base "
metals into silver and gold by the agency of the
Philosopher's Stone.   Merely to remove the evil
sulphur of the "base" metals, thought the alchemists,
though necessary, is not sufficient to transmute them

---

[1] Pseudo-GEBER, whose writings were highly esteemed, for
instance.   See R. RUSSEL's translation of his works (1678),
p. 160.

into " noble " metals ; a maturing process is essential, similar to that which they supposed was effected in Nature's womb. Mystical theology teaches that the powers and life of the soul are not inherent in it, but are given by the free grace of God. Neither, according to the alchemists, are the powers and life of nature in herself, but in that immanent spirit, the Soul of the World, that animates her. As writes the famous alchemist who adopted the pleasing pseudonym of " BASIL VALENTINE " (c. 1600), " the power of growth . . . is imparted not by the earth, but by the life-giving spirit that is in it. If the earth were deserted by this spirit, it would be dead, and no longer able to afford nourishment to anything. For its sulphur or richness would lack the quickening spirit without which there can be neither life nor growth." [1] To perfect the metals, therefore, the alchemists argued, from analogy with mystical theology, which teaches that men can be regenerated only by the power of CHRIST within the soul, that it is necessary to subject them to the action of this world-spirit, this one essence underlying all the varied powers of nature, this One Thing from which " all things were produced . . . by adaption, and which is the cause of all perfection throughout the whole world." [2] " This," writes one alchemist, " is the Spirit of Truth, which the world cannot comprehend without the interposition of the Holy Ghost, or without the instruction of those who know

---

[1] BASIL VALENTINE : *The Twelve Keys*. (See *The Hermetic Museum,* vol. i. pp. 333 and 334.)

[2] From the " Smaragdine Table," attributed to HERMES TRISMEGISTOS (*ie.* MERCURY or THOTH).

it. The same is of a mysterious nature, wondrous strength, boundless power. . . . By Avicenna this Spirit is named the Soul of the World. For, as the Soul moves all the limbs of the Body, so also does this Spirit move all bodies. And as the Soul is in all the limbs of the Body, so also is this Spirit in all elementary created things. It is sought by many and found by few. It is beheld from afar and found near; for it exists in every thing, in every place, and at all times. It has the powers of all creatures; its action is found in all elements, and the qualities of all things are therein, even in the highest perfection . . . it heals all dead and living bodies without other medicine . . . converts all metallic bodies into gold, and there is nothing like unto it under Heaven." [1] It was this Spirit, concentrated in all its potency in a suitable material form, which the alchemists sought under the name of " the Philosopher's Stone ". Now, mystical theology teaches that the Spirit of CHRIST, by which alone the soul of man can be tinctured and transmuted into the likeness of God, is Goodness itself; consequently, the alchemists argued that the Philosopher's Stone must be, so to speak, Gold itself, or the very essence of Gold : it was to them, as CHRIST is of the soul's perfection, at once the pattern and the means of metallic perfection. " The Philosopher's Stone," declares " EIRENÆUS PHILA-LETHES " (*nat. c.* 1623), " is a certain heavenly,

---

[1] *The Book of the Revelation of* HERMES, *interpreted by* THEO-PHRASTUS PARACELSUS, *concerning the Supreme Secret of the World.* (See BENEDICTUS FIGULUS, *A Golden and Blessed Casket of Nature's Marvels,* trans. by A. E. WAITE, 1893, pp. 36, 37, and 41.)

spiritual, penetrative, and fixed substance, which brings all metals to the perfection of gold or silver (according to the quality of the Medicine), and that by natural methods, which yet in their effects transcend Nature. . . . Know, then, that it is called a stone, not because it is like a stone, but only because, by virtue of its fixed nature, it resists the action of fire as successfully as any stone. In species it is gold, more pure than the purest ; it is fixed and incombustible like a stone [*i.e.* it contains no outward sulphur, but only inward, fixed sulphur], but its appearance is that of a very fine powder, impalpable to the touch, sweet to the taste, fragrant to the smell, in potency a most penetrative spirit, apparently dry and yet unctuous, and easily capable of tingeing a plate of metal. . . . If we say that its nature is spiritual, it would be no more than the truth ; if we described it as corporeal the expression would be equally correct ; for it is subtle, penetrative, glorified, spiritual gold. It is the noblest of all created things after the rational soul, and has virtue to repair all defects both in animal and metallic bodies, by restoring them to the most exact and perfect temper ; wherefore is it a spirit or ' quintessence.' " [1]

In other accounts the Philosopher's Stone, or at least the *materia prima* of which it is compounded, is spoken of as a despised substance, reckoned to be of no value. Thus, according to one curious alchemistic work, " This matter, so precious by the excellent Gifts, wherewith Nature has enriched it, is truly mean, with regard to the Substances from

[1] EIRENÆUS PHILALETHES: *A Brief Guide to the Celestial Ruby.* (See *The Hermetic Museum,* vol. ii. pp. 246 and 249.)

whence it derives its Original. Their price is not above the Ability of the Poor. Ten Pence is more than sufficient to purchase the Matter of the Stone. . . . The matter therefore is mean, considering the Foundation of the Art because it costs very little ; it is no less mean, if one considers exteriourly that which gives it Perfection, since in that regard it costs nothing at all, in as much as *all the World has it in its Power* . . . so that . . . it is a constant Truth, that the Stone is a Thing mean in one Sense, but that in another it is most precious, and that there are none but Fools that despise it, by a just Judgment of God." [1]   And JACOB BOEHME (1575–1624) writes : " The *philosopher's stone* is a very dark, disesteemed stone, of a grey colour, but therein lieth the highest tincture." [2]   In these passages there is probably some reference to the ubiquity of the Spirit of the World, already referred to in a former quotation. But this fact is not, in itself, sufficient to account for them. I suggest that their origin is to be found in the religious doctrine that God's Grace, the Spirit of CHRIST that is the means of the transmutation of man's soul into spiritual gold, is free to all ; that it is, at once, the meanest and the most precious thing in the whole Universe. Indeed, I think it quite probable that the alchemists who penned the above-quoted passages had in mind the words of ISAIAH, " He was despised and we esteemed him not." And

---

[1] *A Discourse between Eudoxus and Pyrophilus, upon the Ancient War of the Knights.* See *The Hermetical Triumph : or, the Victorious Philosophical Stone* (1723), pp. 101 and 102.

[2] JACOB BOEHME : *Epistles* (trans. by J. E., 1649, reprinted 1886), Ep. iv., § 111.

if further evidence is required that the alchemists believed in a correspondence between CHRIST—" the Stone which the builders rejected "—and the Philosopher's Stone, reference may be made to the alchemical work called *The Sophic Hydrolith : or Water Stone of the Wise*, a tract included in *The Hermetic Museum*, in which this supposed correspondence is explicitly asserted and dealt with in some detail.

Apart from the alchemists' belief in the analogy between natural and spiritual things, it is, I think, incredible that any such theories of the metals and the possibility of their transmutation or " regeneration " by such an extraordinary agent as the Philosopher's Stone would have occurred to the ancient investigators of Nature's secrets. When they had started to formulate these theories, facts [1] were dis-

---

[1] One of those facts, amongst many others, that appeared to confirm the alchemical doctrines, was the ease with which iron could apparently be transmuted into copper. It was early observed that iron vessels placed in contact with a solution of blue vitriol became converted (at least, so far as their surfaces were concerned) into copper. This we now know to be due to the fact that the copper originally contained in the vitriol is thrown out of solution, whilst the iron takes its place. And we know, also, that no more copper can be obtained in this way from the blue vitriol than is actually used up in preparing it ; and, further, that all the iron which is apparently converted into copper can be got out of the residual solution by appropriate methods, if such be desired; so that the facts really support DALTON'S theory rather than the alchemical doctrines. But to the alchemist it looked like a real transmutation of iron into copper, confirmation of his fond belief that iron and other base metals could be transmuted into silver and gold by the aid of the Great Arcanum of Nature.

covered which appeared to support them ; but it is,
I suggest, practically impossible to suppose that any
or all of these facts would, in themselves, have been
sufficient to give rise to such wonderfully fantastic
theories as these : it is only from the standpoint of
the theory that alchemy was a direct offspring of
mysticism that its origin seems to be capable of
explanation.

In all the alchemical doctrines mystical connec-
tions are evident, and mystical origins can generally
be traced. I shall content myself here with giving
a couple of further examples. Consider, in the
first place, the alchemical doctrine of purification
by putrefaction, that the metals must die before
they can be resurrected and truly live, that through
death alone are they purified—in the more prosaic
language of modern chemistry, death becomes
oxidation, and rebirth becomes reduction. In many
alchemical books there are to be found pictorial
symbols of the putrefaction and death of metals
and their new birth in the state of silver or gold, or
as the Stone itself, together with descriptions of these
processes. The alchemists sought to kill or destroy
the body or outward form of the metals, in the hope
that they might get at and utilise the living essence
they believed to be immanent within. As PARA-
CELSUS put it : " Nothing of true value is located in
the body of a substance, but in the virtue . . . the
less there is of body, the more in proportion is the
virtue." It seems to me quite obvious that in such
ideas as these we have the application to metallurgy
of the mystic doctrine of self-renunciation—that the
soul must die to self before it can live to God ; that

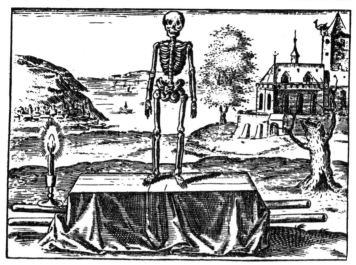

Fig. 41.

Fig. 42.

Symbolical Representations of the Alchemical Principle of Purification
by Putrefaction, from " Basil Valentine's " *Twelve Keys.*

the body must be sacrificed to the spirit, and the individual will bowed down utterly to the One Divine Will, before it can become one therewith.

In the second place, consider the directions as to the colours that must be obtained in the preparation of the Philosopher's Stone, if a successful issue to the Great Work is desired. Such directions are frequently given in considerable detail in alchemical works ; and, without asserting any exact uniformity, I think that I may state that practically all the alchemists agree that three great colour-stages are necessary—(i.) an inky blackness, which is termed the " Crow's Head " and is indicative of putrefaction ; (ii.) a white colour indicating that the Stone is now capable of converting " base " metals into silver ; this passes through orange into (iii.) a red colour, which shows that the Stone is now perfect, and will transmute " base " metals into gold. Now, what was the reason for the belief in these three colour-stages, and for their occurrence in the above order ? I suggest that no alchemist actually obtained these colours in this order in his chemical experiments, and that we must look for a speculative origin for the belief in them. We have, I think, only to turn to religious mysticism for this origin. For the exponents of religious mysticism unanimously agree to a threefold division of the life of the mystic. The first stage is called " the dark night of the soul," wherein it seems as if the soul were deserted by God, although He is very near. It is the time of trial, when self is sacrificed as a duty and not as a delight. Afterwards, however, comes the morning light of a new intelligence, which marks the com-

mencement of that stage of the soul's upward progress that is called the " illuminative life ". All the
mental powers are now concentrated on God, and
the struggle is transferred from without to the inner
man, good works being now done, as it were, spontaneously. The disciple, in this stage, not only
does unselfish deeds, but does them from unselfish
motives, being guided by the light of Divine Truth.
The third stage, which is the consummation of the
process, is termed " the contemplative life ". It is
barely describable. The disciple is wrapped about
with the Divine Love, and is united thereby with
his Divine Source. It is the life of love, as the illuminative life is that of wisdom. I suggest that the alchemists, believing in this threefold division of the
regenerative process, argued that there must be three
similar stages in the preparation of the Stone, which
was the pattern of all metallic perfection ; and that
they derived their beliefs concerning the colours,
and other peculiarities of each stage in the supposed
chemical process, from the characteristics of each
stage in the psychological process according to
mystical theology.

Moreover, in the course of the latter process many
flitting thoughts and affections arise and deeds are
half-wittingly done which are not of the soul's true
character ; and in entire agreement with this, we
read of the alchemical process, in the highly esteemed
" Canons " of D'ESPAGNET : " Besides these decre-
tory signs [i.e. the black, white, orange, and red
colours] which firmly inhere in the matter, and shew
its essential mutations, almost infinite colours appear,
and shew themselves in vapours, as the Rainbow in

the clouds, which quickly pass away and are expelled by those that succeed, more affecting the air than the earth : the operator must have a gentle care of them, because they are not permanent, and proceed not from the intrinsic disposition of the matter, but from the fire painting and fashioning everything after its pleasure, or casually by heat in slight moisture." [1] That D'Espagnet is arguing, not so much from actual chemical experiments, as from analogy with psychological processes in man, is, I think, evident.

As well as a metallic, the alchemists believed in a physiological, application of the fundamental doctrines of mysticism : their physiology was analogically connected with their metallurgy, the same principles holding good in each case. Paracelsus, as we have seen, taught that man is a microcosm, a world in miniature ; his spirit, the Divine Spark within, is from God ; his soul is from the Stars, extracted from the Spirit of the World ; and his body is from the earth, extracted from the elements of which all things material are made. This view of man was shared by many other alchemists. The Philosopher's Stone, therefore (or, rather, a solution of it in alcohol) was also regarded as the Elixir of Life ; which, thought the alchemists, would not endow man with physical immortality, as is sometimes supposed, but restore him again to the flower of youth, " regenerating " him physiologically. Failing this, of course, they regarded gold in a potable

---

[1] Jean D'Espagnet: *Hermetic Arcanum*, canon 65. (See *Collectanea Hermetica*, ed. by W. Wynn Westcott, vol. i., 1893, pp. 28 and 29.)

form as the next most powerful medicine—a belief which probably led to injurious effects in some cases.

Such are the facts from which I think we are justified in concluding, as I have said, " that the alchemists constructed their chemical theories for the main part by means of *a priori* reasoning, and that the premises from which they started were (i.) the truth of mystical theology, especially the doctrine of the soul's regeneration, and (ii.) the truth of mystical philosophy, which asserts that the objects of nature are symbols of spiritual verities."[1]

It seems to follow, *ex hypothesi*, that every alchemical work ought to permit of two interpretations, one physical, the other transcendental. But I would not venture to assert this, because, as I think, many of the lesser alchemists knew little of the origin of their theories, nor realised their significance. They were concerned merely with these theories in their strictly metallurgical applications, and any transcendental meaning we can extract from their works was not intended by the writers themselves. However, many alchemists, I conceive, especially the better sort, realised more or less clearly the dual nature of their subject, and their books are to some extent intended to permit of a double interpretation, although the emphasis is laid upon the physical and chemical application of mystical doctrine. And there are a few writers who adopted alchemical terminology on the principle that, if the language of theology

[1] In the following excursion we will wander again in the alchemical bypaths of thought, and certain objections to this view of the origin and nature of alchemy will be dealt with and, I hope, satisfactorily answered.

is competent to describe chemical processes, then, conversely, the language of alchemy must be competent to describe psychological processes : this is certainly and entirely true of JACOB BOEHME, and, to some extent also, I think, of HENRY KHUNRATH (1560–1605) and THOMAS VAUGHAN (1622–1666).

As may be easily understood, many of the alchemists led most romantic lives, often running the risk of torture and death at the hands of avaricious princes who believed them to be in possession of the Philosopher's Stone, and adopted such pleasant methods of extorting (or, at least, of trying to extort) their secrets. A brief sketch, which I quote from my *Alchemy : Ancient and Modern* (1911), § 54, of the lives of ALEXANDER SETHON and MICHAEL SENDIVOGIUS, will serve as an example :—

" The date and birthplace of ALEXANDER SETHON, a Scottish alchemist, do not appear to have been recorded, but MICHAEL SENDIVOGIUS was probably born in Moravia about 1566. Sethon, we are told, was in possession of the arch-secrets of Alchemy. He visited Holland in 1602, proceeded after a time to Italy, and passed through Basle to Germany ; meanwhile he is said to have performed many transmutations. Ultimately arriving at Dresden, however, he fell into the clutches of the young Elector, Christian II., who, in order to extort his secret, cast him into prison and put him to the torture, but without avail. Now it so happened that Sendivogius, who was in quest of the Philosopher's Stone, was staying at Dresden, and hearing of Sethon's imprisonment obtained permission to visit him. Sendivogius offered to effect Sethon's escape in return for assistance in his alchemistic pursuits, to which arrangement the Scottish alchemist willingly agreed. After some considerable outlay of money in bribery, Sendivogius's plan of escape was successfully carried out, and Sethon found himself a free man ; but he refused to betray the high secrets of Hermetic philosophy to his rescuer. However, before his death, which occurred shortly afterwards, he presented him with an ounce of the transmutative powder. Sendivogius soon used up this powder, we are told, in effecting transmutations and cures, and, being fond of expensive living, he married Sethon's widow, in the hope that she was in the possession of the transmutative secret. In this, however, he was disappointed ; she knew nothing of the matter, but she had the manuscript of an alchemistic work written by her late husband. Shortly afterwards Sendivogius printed at Prague a book entitled *The New Chemical Light* under the name of ' Cosmopolita,' which is said to have been this work of Sethon's, but which Sendivogius claimed for his own by the insertion of his name on the title page, in the form of an anagram. The tract *On Sulphur* which was printed at the end of the book in later editions, however, is said to have been the genuine work of the Moravian. Whilst his powder lasted, Sendivogius travelled about, performing, we are told, many transmutations. He was twice imprisoned in order to extort the secrets of alchemy from him, on one occasion escaping, and on the other occasion obtaining his release from the Emperor Rudolph. Afterwards, he appears to have degenerated into an impostor, but this is said to have been a *finesse* to hide his true character as an alchemistic adept. He died in 1646."

However, all the alchemists were not of the apparent character of SENDIVOGIUS—many of them leading holy and serviceable lives. The alchemist-physician J. B. VAN HELMONT (1577–1644), who was a man of extraordinary benevolence, going about treating the sick poor freely, may be particularly mentioned. He, too, claimed to have performed the transmutation of "base" metal into gold, as did also HELVETIUS (whom we have already met), physician to the Prince of Orange, with a wonderful preparation given to him by a stranger. The testimony of these two latter men is very difficult either to explain or to explain away, but I cannot deal with this question here, but must refer the reader to a paper on the subject by Mr GASTON DE MENGEL, and the discussion thereon, published in vol. i. of *The Journal of the Alchemical Society*.

In conclusion, I will venture one remark dealing with a matter outside of the present inquiry. Alchemy ended its days in failure and fraud ; charlatans and fools were attracted to it by purely mercenary objects, who knew nothing of the high aims of the genuine alchemists, and scientific men looked elsewhere for solutions of Nature's problems. Why did alchemy fail ? Was it because its fundamental theorems were erroneous ? I think not. I consider the failure of the alchemical theory of Nature to be due rather to the misapplication of these fundamental concepts, to the erroneous use of *a priori* methods of reasoning, to a lack of a sufficiently wide knowledge of natural phenomena to which to apply these concepts, to a lack of adequate apparatus with which to investigate such phenomena experimentally, and to a lack of mathematical organons of thought with which to interpret such experimental results had they been obtained. As for the basic concepts of alchemy themselves, such as the fundamental unity of the Cosmos and the evolution of the elements, in a word, the applicability of the principles of mysticism to natural phenomena : these seem to me to contain a very valuable element of truth—a statement which, I think, modern scientific research justifies me in making,—though the alchemists distorted this truth and expressed it in a fantastic form. I think, indeed, that in the modern theories of energy and the all-pervading ether, the etheric and electrical origin and nature of matter and the evolution of the elements, we may witness the triumphs of mysticism as applied to the interpretation of Nature. Whether or not we shall ever transmute lead into gold, I believe there is a very true sense in which we may say that alchemy, purified by its death, has been proved true, whilst the materialistic view of Nature has been proved false.

X

THE PHALLIC ELEMENT IN ALCHEMICAL DOCTRINE

THE problem of alchemy presents many aspects to our view, but, to my mind, the most fundamental of these is psychological, or, perhaps I should say, epistemological. It has been said that the proper study of mankind is man ; and to study man we must study the beliefs of man. Now so long as we neglect great tracts of such beliefs, because they have been, or appear to have been, superseded, so long will our study be incomplete and ineffectual. And this, let me add, is no mere excuse for the study of alchemy, no mere afterthought put forward in justification of a predilection, but a plain statement of fact that renders this study an imperative need. There are other questions of interest—of very great interest—concerning alchemy : questions, for instance, as to the scope and validity of its doctrines ; but we ought not to allow their fascination and promise to distract our attention from the fundamental problem, whose solution is essential to their elucidation.

In the preceding essay on " The Quest of the Philosopher's Stone," which was written from the standpoint I have sketched in the foregoing words, my thesis was " that the alchemists constructed their chemical theories for the main part by means of *a priori* reasoning, and that the premises from which they started were (i.) the truth of mystical theology, especially the doctrine of the soul's regeneration, and (ii.) the truth of mystical philosophy, which asserts that the objects of nature are symbols of spiritual verities." Now, I wish to treat my present thesis, which is concerned with a further source from which the alchemists derived certain of their views and modes of expression by means of *a priori* reasoning, in connection with, and, in a sense, as complementary to, my former thesis. I propose in the first place, therefore, briefly to deal with certain possible objections to this view of alchemy.

It has, for instance, been maintained [1] that the assimilation of alchemical doctrines concerning the metals to those of mysticism concerning the soul was an event late in the history of alchemy, and was undertaken in the interests of the latter doctrines. Now we know that certain mystics of the sixteenth and seventeenth centuries did borrow from the alchemists much of their terminology with which to discourse of spiritual mysteries—JACOB BOEHME, HENRY KHUNRATH, and perhaps THOMAS VAUGHAN, may be mentioned as the most prominent cases in point. But how was this possible if it were not, as I have suggested, the repayment, in a sense, of a sort of philological debt ? Transmutation was an admirable vehicle of language for describing the

---

[1] See, for example, Mr A. E. WAITE's paper, " The Canon of Criticism in respect of Alchemical Literature," *The Journal of the Alchemical Society*, vol. i. (1913), pp. 17–30.

soul's regeneration, just because the doctrine of transmutation was the result of an attempt to apply the doctrine of regeneration in the sphere of metallurgy ; and similar remarks hold of the other prominent doctrines of alchemy.

The wonderful fabric of alchemical doctrine was not woven in a day, and as it passed from loom to loom, from Byzantium to Syria, from Syria to Arabia, from Arabia to Spain and Latin Europe, so its pattern changed ; but it was always woven *a priori*, in the belief that that which is below is as that which is above. In its final form, I think, it is distinctly Christian.

In the *Turba Philosophorum*, the oldest known work of Latin alchemy—a work which, claiming to be of Greek origin, whilst not that, is certainly Greek in spirit,—we frequently come across statements of a decidedly mystical character. " The regimen," we read, " is greater than is perceived by reason, except through divine inspiration." [1] Copper, it is insisted upon again and again, has a soul as well as a body ; and the Art, we are told, is to be defined as " the liquefaction of the body and the separation of the soul from the body, seeing that copper, like a man, has a soul and a body." [2] Moreover, other doctrines are here propounded which, although not so obviously of a mystical character, have been traced to mystical sources in the preceding excursion. There is, for instance, the doctrine of purification by means of putrefaction, this process being likened

---

[1] *The Turba Philosophorum, or Assembly of the Sages* (trans. by A. E. WAITE, 1896), p. 128.

[2] *Ibid.*, p. 193, *cf.* pp. 102 and 152.

to that of the resurrection of man. " These things being done," we read, " God will restore unto it [the matter operated on] both the soul and the spirit thereof, and the weakness being taken away, that matter will be made strong, and after corruption will be improved, even as a man becomes stronger after resurrection and younger than he was in this world." [1] The three stages in the alchemical work— black, white, and red—corresponding to, and, as I maintain, based on the three stages in the life of the mystic, are also more than once mentioned. " Cook them [the king and his wife], therefore, until they become black, then white, afterwards red, and finally until a tingeing venom is produced." [2]

In view of these quotations, the alliance (shall I say ?) between alchemy and mysticism cannot be asserted to be of late origin. And we shall find similar statements if we go further back in time. To give but one example : " Among the earliest authorities," writes Mr WAITE, " the *Book of Crates* says that copper, like man, has a spirit, soul, and body," the term " copper " being symbolical and applying to a stage in the alchemical work. But nowhere in the *Turba* do we meet with the concept of the Philosopher's Stone as the medicine of the metals, a concept characteristic of Latin alchemy, and, to quote Mr WAITE again, " it does not appear that the conception of the Philosopher's Stone as a medicine of metals and of men was familiar to Greek alchemy." [3]

[1] *The Turba Philosophorum, or Assembly of the Sages* (trans. by A. E. WAITE), p. 101, *cf.* pp. 27 and 197.
[2] *Ibid.*, p. 98, *cf.* p. 29.   [3] *Ibid.*, p. 71.

All this seems to me very strongly to support my view of the origin of alchemy, which requires a specifically Christian mysticism only for this specific concept of the Philosopher's Stone in its fully-fledged form. At any rate, the development of alchemical doctrine can be seen to have proceeded concomitantly with the development of mystical philosophy and theology. Those who are not prepared here to see effect and cause may be asked not only to formulate some other hypothesis in explanation of the origin of alchemy, but also to explain this fact of concomitant development.

From the standpoint of the transcendental theory of alchemy it has been urged " that the language of mystical theology seemed to be hardly so suitable to the exposition [as I maintain] or concealment of chemical theories, as the language of a definite and generally credited branch of science was suited to the expression of a veiled and symbolical process such as the regeneration of man." [1] But such a statement is only possible with respect to the latest days of alchemy, when there *was* a science of chemistry, definite and generally credited. The science of chemistry, it must be remembered, had no growth separate from alchemy, but evolved therefrom. Of the days before this evolution had been accomplished, it would be in closer accord with the facts to say that theology, including the doctrine of man's regeneration, was in the position of " a definite and generally credited branch of science," whereas chemical phenomena were veiled in deepest mystery and tinged with

[1] PHILIP S. WELLBY, M.A., in *The Journal of the Alchemical Society*, vol. ii. (1914), p. 104.

the dangers appertaining to magic. As concerns the origin of alchemy, therefore, the argument as to suitability of language appears to support my own theory ; it being open to assume that after formulation—that is, in alchemy's latter days — chemical nomenclature and theories were employed by certain writers to veil heterodox religious doctrine.

Another recent writer on the subject, my friend the late Mr ABDUL-ALI, has remarked that " he thought that, in the mind of the alchemist at least, there was something more than analogy between metallic and psychic transformations, and that the whole subject might well be assigned to the doctrinal category of ineffable and transcendent Oneness. This Oneness comprehended all—soul and body, spirit and matter, mystic visions and waking life— and the sharp metaphysical distinction between the mental and the non-mental realms, so prominent during the history of philosophy, was not regarded by these early investigators in the sphere of nature. There was the sentiment, perhaps only dimly experienced, that not only the law, but the substance of the Universe, was one ; that mind was everywhere in contact with its own kindred ; and that metallic transmutation would, somehow, so to speak, signalise and seal a hidden transmutation of the soul." [1]

I am to a large extent in agreement with this view. Mr ABDUL-ALI quarrels with the term " analogy," and, if it is held to imply any merely superficial resemblance, it certainly is not adequate to my own needs, though I know not what other

[1] SIJIL ABDUL-ALI, in *The Journal of the Alchemical Society*, vol. ii. (1914), p. 102.

word to use. SWEDENBORG's term "correspondence" would be better for my purpose, as standing for an essential connection between spirit and matter, arising out of the causal relationship of the one to the other. But if SWEDENBORG believed that matter and spirit were most intimately related, he nevertheless had a very precise idea of their distinctness, which he formulated in his Doctrine of Degrees—a very exact metaphysical doctrine indeed. The alchemists, on the other hand, had no such clear ideas on the subject. It would be even more absurd to attribute to them a Cartesian dualism. To their ways of thinking, it was by no means impossible to grasp the spiritual essences of things by what we should now call chemical manipulations. For them a gas was still a ghost and air a spirit. One could quote pages in support of this, but I will content myself with a few words from the *Turba*—the antiquity of the book makes it of value, and anyway it is near at hand. "Permanent water," whatever that may be, being pounded with the body, we are told, "by the will of God it turns that body into spirit." And in another place we read that "the Philosophers have said : Except ye turn bodies into not-bodies, and incorporeal things into bodies, ye have not yet discovered the rule of operation."[1] No one who could write like this, and believe it, could hold matter and spirit as altogether distinct. But it is equally obvious that the injunction to convert body into spirit is meaningless if spirit and body are held to be identical. I have been criticised for crediting the alchemists "with the philosophic acumen of

[1] *Op. cit.*, pp. 65 and 110, *cf.* p. 154.

Hegel," [1] but that is just what I think one ought to
avoid doing. At the same time, however, it is extremely difficult to give a precise account of views
which are very far from being precise themselves.
But I think it may be said, without fear of error,
that the alchemist who could say, " As above, so
below," *ipso facto* recognised both a very close connection between spirit and matter, and a distinction
between them. Moreover, the division thus implied corresponded, on the whole, to that between
the realms of the known (or what was thought to be
known) and the unknown. The Church, whether
Christian or pre-Christian, had very precise (comparatively speaking) doctrine concerning the soul's
origin, duties, and destiny, backed up by tremendous
authority, and speculative philosophy had advanced
very far by the time PLATO began to concern himself
with its problems. Nature, on the other hand, was
a mysterious world of magical happenings, and there
was nothing deserving of the name of natural science
until alchemy was becoming decadent. It is not
surprising, therefore, that the alchemists—these men
who wished to probe Nature's hidden mysteries—
should reason from above to below ; indeed, unless
they had started *de novo*—as babes knowing nothing,
—there was no other course open to them. And that
they did adopt the obvious course is all that my
former thesis amounts to. In passing, it is interesting to note that a sixteenth-century alchemist, who
had exceptional opportunities and leisure to study
the works of the old masters of alchemy, seems to

---

[1] *Vide* a rather frivolous review of my *Alchemy: Ancient
and Modern* in *The Outlook* for 14th January 1911.

have come to a similar conclusion as to the nature of their reasoning. He writes : " The Sages . . . after having conceived in their minds a Divine idea of the relations of the whole universe . . . selected from among the rest a certain substance, from which they sought to elicit the elements, to separate and purify them, and then again put them together in a manner suggested by a keen and profound observation of Nature." [1]

In describing the realm of spirit as *ex hypothesi* known, that of Nature unknown, to the alchemists, I have made one important omission, and that, if I may use the name of a science to denominate a complex of crude facts, is the realm of physiology, which, falling within that of Nature, must yet be classed as *ex hypothesi* known. But to elucidate this point some further considerations are necessary touching the general nature of knowledge. Now, facts may be roughly classed, according to their obviousness and frequency of occurrence, into four groups. There are, first of all, facts which are so obvious, to put it paradoxically, that they escape notice ; and these facts are the commonest and most frequent in their occurrence. I think it is Mr CHESTERTON who has said that, looking at a forest one cannot see the trees because of the forest ; and, in *The Innocence of Father Brown*, he has a good story (" The Invisible Man ") illustrating the point, in which a man renders himself invisible by dressing up in a postman's uniform. At any rate, we know that when a

[1] EDWARD KELLY : *The Humid Path.* (See *The Alchemical Writings of* EDWARD KELLY, edited by A. E. WAITE, 1893, pp. 59–60.)

phenomenon becomes persistent it tends to escape observation ; thus, continuous motion can only be appreciated with reference to a stationary body, and a noise, continually repeated, becomes at last inaudible. The tendency of often-repeated actions to become habitual, and at last automatic, that is to say, carried out without consciousness, is a closely related phenomenon. We can understand, therefore, why a knowledge of the existence of the atmosphere, as distinct from the wind, came late in the history of primitive man, as, also, many other curious gaps in his knowledge. In the second group we may put those facts which are common, that is, of frequent occurrence, and are classed as obvious. Such facts are accepted at face-value by the primitive mind, and are used as the basis of explanation of facts in the two remaining groups, namely, those facts which, though common, are apt to escape the attention owing to their inconspicuousness, and those which are of infrequent occurrence. When the mind takes the trouble to observe a fact of the third group, or is confronted by one of the fourth, it feels a sense of surprise. Such facts wear an air of strangeness, and the mind can only rest satisfied when it has shown them to itself as in some way cases of the second group of facts, or, at least, brought them into relation therewith. That is what the mind—at least the primitive mind—means by " explanation ". " It is obvious," we say, commencing an argument, thereby proclaiming our intention to bring that which is at first in the category of the not-obvious, into the category of the obvious. It remains for a more sceptical type of mind—a later product of human evolution—to question obvious facts, to explain them, either, as in science, by establishing deeper and more far-reaching correlations between phenomena, or in philosophy, by seeking for the source and purpose of such facts, or, better still, by both methods.

Of the second class of facts—those common and obvious facts which the primitive mind accepts at face-value and uses as the basis of its explanations of such things as seem to it to stand in need of explanation—one could hardly find a better instance than sex. The universality of sex, and the intermittent character of its phenomena, are both responsible for this. Indeed, the attitude of mind I have referred to is not restricted to primitive man ; how many people to-day, for instance, just accept sex as a fact, pleasant or unpleasant according to their predilections, never querying, or feeling the need to query, its why and wherefore ? It is by no means surprising, that when man first felt the need of satisfying himself as to the origin of the universe, he should have done so by a theory founded on what he knew of his own generation. Indeed, as I queried on a former occasion, what other source of explanation was open to him ? Of what other form of origin was he aware ? Seeing Nature springing to life at the kiss of the sun, what more natural than that she should be regarded as the divine Mother, who bears fruits because impregnated by the Sun-God ? It is not difficult to understand, therefore, why primitive man paid divine honours to the organs of sex in man and woman, or to such things as he considered symbolical of them—that is to say, to understand the extensiveness of those religions which are grouped under the term " phallicism ". Nor, to my mind, is the symbol of sex a wholly inadequate one under which to conceive of the origin of things. And, as I have said before, that phallicism usually appears to have degenerated into immorality of a very pronounced type is to be deplored, but an immoral view of human relations is by no means a necessary corollary to a sexual theory of the universe.[1]

[1] " The reverence as well as the worship paid to the phallus, in early and primitive days, had nothing in it which partook of indecency ; all ideas connected with it were of a reverential and religious kind. . . .

" The indecent ideas attached to the representation of the phallus were, though it seems a paradox to say so, the results of a more advanced civilization verging towards its decline, as we have evidence at Rome and Pompeii. . . .

" To the primitive man [the reproductive force which pervades all nature] was the most mysterious of all manifestations. The visible physical powers of nature—the sun, the sky, the storm—naturally claimed his reverence, but to him the generative power was the most mysterious of all powers. In the vegetable world, the live seed placed in the ground, and hence germinating, sprouting up, and becoming a beautiful and umbrageous tree, was a mystery. In the animal world, as the cause of all life, by which all beings came into existence, this power was a mystery. In the view of primitive man generation was the action of the Deity itself. It was the mode in which He brought all things into existence, the sun, the moon, the stars, the world, man were generated by Him. To the productive power man was deeply indebted, for to it he owed the harvests and the flocks which supported his life ; hence it naturally became an object of reverence and worship.

" Primitive man wants some object to worship, for an abstract idea is beyond his comprehension, hence a visible representation of the generative Deity was made, with the organs contributing to generation most prominent, and hence

The Aruntas of Australia, I believe, when discovered by Europeans, had not yet observed the connection between sexual intercourse and birth. They believed that conception was occasioned by the woman passing near a *churinga*—a peculiarly shaped piece of wood or stone, in which a spirit-child was concealed, which entered into her. But archæological research having established the fact that phallicism has, at one time or another, been common to nearly all races, it seems probable that the Arunta tribe represents a deviation from the normal line of mental evolution. At any rate, an isolated phenomenon, such as this, cannot be held to controvert the view that regards phallicism as in this normal line. Nor was the attitude of mind that not only accepts sex at face-value as an obvious fact, but uses the concept of it to explain other facts, a merely transitory one. We may, indeed, not difficultly trace it throughout the history of alchemy, giving rise to what I may term " The Phallic Element in Alchemical Doctrine ".

In aiming to establish this, I may be thought to be endeavouring to establish a counter-thesis to that of the preceding essay on alchemy, but, in virtue of the alchemists' belief in the mystical unity of all things, in the analogical or correspondential relationship of all parts of the universe to each other, the mystical and the phallic views of the origin of alchemy are complementary, not antagonistic. Indeed, the assumption that the metals are the symbols of man

the organ itself became a symbol of the power."—H. M. WESTROPP: *Primitive Symbolism as Illustrated in Phallic Worship, or the Reproductive Principle* (1885), pp. 47, 48, and 57.

almost necessitates the working out of physiological as well as mystical analogies, and these two series of analogies are themselves connected, because the principle " As above, so below " was held to be true of man himself. We might, therefore, expect to find a more or less complete harmony between the two series of symbols, though, as a matter of fact, contradictions will be encountered when we come to consider points of detail. The undoubtable antiquity of the phallic element in alchemical doctrine precludes the idea that this element was an adventitious one, that it was in any sense an afterthought ; notwithstanding, however, the evidence, as will, I hope, become apparent as we proceed, indicates that mystical ideas played a much more fundamental part in the genesis of alchemical doctrine than purely phallic ones—mystical interpretations fit alchemical processes and theories far better than do sexual interpretations ; in fact, sex has to be interpreted somewhat mystically in order to work out the analogies fully and satisfactorily.

As concerns Greek alchemy, I shall content myself with a passage from a work *On the Sacred Art*, attributed to OLYMPIODORUS (sixth century A.D.), followed by some quotations from and references to the *Turba*. In the former work it is stated on the authority of HORUS that " The proper end of the whole art is to obtain the semen of the male secretly, seeing that all things are male and female. Hence [we read further] Horus says in a certain place : Join the male and the female, and you will find that which is sought ; as a fact, without this process of re-union, nothing can succeed, for Nature

charms Nature," *etc.* The *Turba* insistently commands those who would succeed in the Art, to conjoin the male with the female,[1] and, in one place,
the male is said to be lead and the female orpiment.[2]
We also find the alchemical work symbolised by the
growth of the embryo in the womb. " Know," we
are told, " . . . that out of the elect things nothing
becomes useful without conjunction and regimen,
because sperma is generated out of blood and desire.
For the man mingling with the woman, the sperm
is nourished by the humour of the womb, and by
the moistening blood, and by heat, and when forty
nights have elapsed the sperm is formed. . . . God
has constituted that heat and blood for the nourishment of the sperm until the fœtus is brought forth.
So long as it is little, it is nourished with milk, and
in proportion as the vital heat is maintained, the
bones are strengthened. Thus it behoves you also
to act in this Art."[3]

The use of the mystical symbols of death (putrefaction) and resurrection or rebirth to represent
the consummation of the alchemical work, and that
of the phallic symbols of the conjunction of the sexes
and the development of the fœtus, both of which we
have found in the *Turba*, are current throughout the
course of Latin alchemy. In *The Chymical Marriage
of Christian Rosencreutz*, that extraordinary document
of what is called " Rosicrucianism "—a symbolic
romance of considerable ability, whoever its author

---

[1] *Vide* pp. 60, 92, 96, 97, 134, 135 and elsewhere in Mr
WAITE's translation.

[2] *Ibid.*, p. 57.

[3] *Ibid.*, pp. 179–181 (second recension); *cf.* pp. 103–104.

was,[1]—an attempt is made to weld the two sets of symbols—the one of marriage, the other of death and resurrection unto glory—into one allegorical narrative ; and it is to this fusion of seemingly disparate concepts that much of its fantasticality is due. Yet the concepts are not really disparate ; for not only is the second birth like unto the first, and not only is the resurrection unto glory described as the Bridal Feast of the Lamb, but marriage is, in a manner, a form of death and rebirth. To justify this in a crude sense, I might say that, from the male standpoint at least, it is a giving of the life-substance to the beloved that life may be born anew and increase. But in a deeper sense it is, or rather should be, as an ideal, a mutual sacrifice of self for each other's good—a death of the self that it may arise with an enriched personality.

It is when we come to an examination of the ideas at the root of, and associated with, the alchemical concept of " principles," that we find some difficulty in harmonising the two series of symbols—the mystical and the phallic. In one place in the *Turba* we are directed " to take quicksilver, in which is the male potency or strength " ;[2] and this concept of mercury as male is quite in accord with the mystical origin I have assigned in the preceding excursion to the doctrine of the alchemical principles. I have shown, I think, that salt, sulphur, and mercury are the analogues *ex hypothesi* of the body, soul (affection and volition), and spirit (intelligence or understand-

---

[1] See Mr WAITE's *The Real History of the Rosicrucians* (1887) for translation and discussion as to origin and significance. The work was first published (in German) at Strassburg in 1616.   [2] Mr WAITE's translation, p. 79.

ing) in man ; and the affections are invariably regarded as especially feminine, the understanding as especially masculine. But it seems that the more common opinion, amongst Latin alchemists at any rate, was that sulphur was male and mercury female. Writes BERNARD of TRÉVISAN : " For the Matter suffereth, and the Form acteth assimulating the Matter to itself, and according to this manner the Matter naturally thirsteth after a Form, as a Woman desireth an Husband, and a Vile thing a precious one, and an impure a pure one, so also *Argent-vive* coveteth a Sulphur, as that which should make perfect which is imperfect : So also a Body freely desireth a Spirit, whereby it may at length arrive at its perfection."[1] At the same time, however, Mercury was regarded as containing in itself both male and female potencies —it was the product of male and female, and, thus, the seed of all the metals. " Nothing in the World can be generated," to repeat a quotation from BERNARD, " without these two Substances, to wit a Male and Female : From whence it appeareth, that although these two substances are not of one and the same species, yet one Stone doth thence arise, and although they appear and are said to be two Substances, yet in truth it is but one, to wit, *Argent-vive*. But of this *Argent-vive* a certain part is fixed and digested, Masculine, hot, dry and secretly informing. But the other, which is the Female, is volatile, crude, cold, and moyst."[2] EDWARD KELLY

---

[1] BERNARD, Earl of TRÉVISAN : *A Treatise of the Philosopher's Stone*, 1683. (See *Collectanea Chymica : A Collection of Ten Several Treatises in Chymistry*, 1684, p. 92.)

[2] *Ibid.*, p. 91.

(1555–1595), who is valuable because he summarises authoritative opinion, says somewhat the same thing, though in clearer words : " The active elements . . . these are water and fire . . . may be called male, while the passive elements . . . earth and air . . . represent the female principle. . . . Only two elements, water and earth, are visible, and earth is called the hiding-place of fire, water the abode of air. In these two elements we have the broad law of limitation which divides the male from the female. . . . The first matter of minerals is a kind of viscous water, mingled with pure and impure earth. . . . Of this viscous water and fusible earth, or sulphur, is composed that which is called quicksilver, the first matter of the metals. Metals are nothing but Mercury digested by different degrees of heat." [1] There is one difference, however, between these two writers, inasmuch as BERNARD says that " the Male and Female abide together in closed Natures ; the Female truly as it were Earth and Water, the Male as Air and Fire." Mercury for him arises from the two former elements, sulphur from the two latter.[2] And the difference is important as showing beyond question the *a priori* nature of alchemical reasoning. The idea at the back of the alchemists' minds was undoubtedly that of the ardour of the male in the act of coition and the alleged, or perhaps I should

[1] EDWARD KELLY : *The Stone of the Philosophers.* (See *The Alchemical Writings of* EDWARD KELLY, edited by A. E. WAITE, 1893, pp. 9 and 11 to 13.)

[2] *The Answer of* BERNARDUS TREVISANUS, *to the Epistle of Thomas of Bononia, Physician to K. Charles the 8th.* (See JOHN FREDERICK HOUPREGHT : *Aurifontina Chymica,* 1680, p. 208.)

say apparent, passivity of the female. Consequently, sulphur, the fiery principle of combustion, and such elements as were reckoned to be active, were denominated " male," whilst mercury, the principle acted on by sulphur, and such elements as were reckoned to be passive, were denominated " female ". As to the question of origin, I do not think that the palm can be denied to the mystical as distinguished from the phallic theory. And in its final form the doctrine of principles is incapable of a sexual interpretation. Mystically understood, man is capable of analysis into two principles—since " body " may be neglected as unimportant (a false view, I think, by the way) or " soul " and " spirit " may be united under one head—*or* into three ; whereas the postulation of *three* principles on a sexual basis is impossible. Joannes Isaacus Hollandus (fifteenth century) is the earliest author in whose works I have observed explicit mention of *three* principles, though he refers to them in a manner seeming to indicate that the doctrine was no new one in his day. I have only read one little tract of his ; there is nothing sexual in it, and the author's mental character may be judged from his remarks concerning " the three flying spirits "—taste, smell, and colour. These, he writes, " are the life, soule, and quintessence of every thing, neither can these three spirits be one without the other, as the Father, the Son, and the Holy Ghost are one, yet three Persons, and one is not without the other." [1]

---

[1] *One Hundred and Fourteen Experiments and Cures of the Famous Physitian* Theophrastus Paracelsus. *Whereunto is added . . . certain Secrets of* Isaac Hollandus, *concerning the Vegetall and Animall Work* (1652), pp. 29 and 30.

When the alchemists described an element or principle as male or female, they meant what they said, as I have already intimated, to the extent, at least, of firmly believing that seed was produced by the two metallic sexes. By their union metals were thought to be produced in the womb of the earth ; and mines were shut in order that by the birth and growth of new metal the impoverished veins might be replenished. In this way, too, was the *magnum opus*, the generation of the Philosopher's Stone—in species gold, but purer than the purest—to be accomplished. To conjoin that which Nature supplied, to foster the growth and development of that which was thereby produced ; such was the task of the alchemist. " For there are Vegetables," says BERNARD of TRÉVISAN in his *Answer to Thomas of Bononia,* " but Sensitives more especially, which for the most part beget their like, by the Seeds of the Male and Female for the most part concurring and conmixt by copulation ; which work of Nature the Philosophick Art imitates in the generation of gold." [1]

Mercury, as I have said, was commonly regarded as the seed of the metals, or as especially the female seed, there being two seeds, one the male, according to BERNARD, " more ripe, perfect and active," the other the female. " more immature and in a sort passive.[2] " . . . our Philosophick Art," he says in another place, following a description of the generation of man, " . . . is like this procreation of Man ; for as in *Mercury* (of which Gold is by Nature generated in Mineral Vessels) a natural conjunction

[1] *Op. cit.,* p. 216. [2] *Ibid.,* p. 217 ; *cf.* p. 236.

is made of both the Seeds, Male and Female, so by our artifice, an artificial and like conjunction is made of Agents and Patients." [1] " All teaching," says KELLY, " that changes Mercury is false and vain, for this is the original sperm of metals, and its moisture must not be dried up, for otherwise it will not dissolve," [2] and quotes ARNOLD (*ob. c.* 1310) to a similar effect.[3] One wonders how far the fact that human and animal seed is fluid influenced the alchemists in their choice of mercury, the only metal liquid at ordinary temperatures, as the seed of the metals. There are, indeed, other good reasons for this choice, but that this idea played some part in it, and, at least, was present at the back of the alchemists' minds, I have little doubt.

The most philosophic account of metallic seed is that, perhaps, of the mysterious adept " EIRENÆUS PHILALETHES," who distinguishes between it and mercury in a rather interesting manner. He writes : " Seed is the means of generic propagation given to all perfect things here below ; it is the perfection of each body ; and anybody that has no seed must be regarded as imperfect. Hence there can be no doubt that there is such a thing as metallic seed. . . . All metallic seed is the seed of gold ; for gold is the intention of Nature in regard to all metals. If the base metals are not gold, it is only through some accidental hindrance ; they are all potentially gold. But, of course, this seed of gold is most easily obtainable from well-matured gold itself. . . . Remember that I am now speaking of metallic seed, and not of

---

[1] *The Answer of* BERNARDUS TREVISANUS, *etc. Op. cit.,* p. 218.　　[2] *Op. cit.,* p. 22.　　[3] *Ibid.,* p. 16.

Mercury. . . . The seed of metals is hidden out of sight still more completely than that of animals ; nevertheless, it is within the compass of our Art to extract it. The seed of animals and vegetables is something separate, and may be cut out, or otherwise separately exhibited ; but metallic seed is diffused throughout the metal, and contained in all its smallest parts ; neither can it be discerned from its body : its extraction is therefore a task which may well tax the ingenuity of the most experienced philosopher ; the virtues of the whole metal have to be intensified, so as to convert it into the sperm of our seed, which, by circulation, receives the virtues of superiors and inferiors, then next becomes wholly form, or heavenly virtue, which can communicate this to others related to it by homogeneity of matter. . . . The place in which the seed resides is—approximately speaking—water ; for, to speak properly and exactly, the seed is the smallest part of the metal, and is invisible ; but as this invisible presence is diffused throughout the water of its kind, and exerts its virtue therein, nothing being visible to the eye but water, we are left to conclude from rational induction that this inward agent (which is, properly speaking, the seed) is really there. Hence we call the whole of the water seed, just as we call the whole of the grain seed, though the germ of life is only a smallest particle of the grain." [1]

To say that " PHILALETHES' " seed resembles the modern electron is, perhaps, to draw a rather fanciful analogy, since the electron is a very precise idea, the

[1] EIRENÆUS PHILALETHES: *The Metamorphosis of Metals.* (See *The Hermetic Museum,* vol. ii. pp. 238–240.)

Fig. 43.

Symbolic Alchemical Design illustrating the Conjunction of Brother and Sister, from Michael Maier's *Atalanta Fugiens* (1617).

(By permission of the British Museum.　Photo by Donald Macbeth, London.)

result of the mathematical interpretation of the results of exact experimentation. But though it would be absurd to speak of this concept of the one seed of all metals as an anticipation of the electron, to apply the expression " metallic seed " to the electron, now that the concept of it has been reached, does not seem so absurd.

According to " PHILALETHES," the extraction of the seed is a very difficult process, accomplishable, however, by the aid of mercury—the water homogeneous therewith. Mercury, again, is the form of the seed thereby obtained. He writes : " When the sperm hidden in the body of gold is brought out by means of our Art, it appears under the form of Mercury, whence it is exalted into the quintessence which is first white, and then, by means of continuous coction, becomes red." And again : " There is a womb into which the gold (if placed therein) will, of its own accord, emit its seed, until it is debilitated and dies, and by its death is renewed into a most glorious King, who thenceforward receives power to deliver all his brethren from the fear of death." [1]

The fifteenth-century alchemist THOMAS NORTON was peculiar in his views, inasmuch as he denied that metals have seed. He writes : " Nature never multiplies anything, except in either one or the other of these two ways : either by decay, which we call putrefaction, or, in the case of animate creatures, by propagation. In the case of metals there can be no propagation, though our Stone exhibits something

---

[1] EIRENÆUS PHILALETHES : *The Metamorphosis of Metals.* (See *The Hermetic Museum,* vol. ii. pp. 241 and 244.)

like it. . . . Nothing can be multiplied by inward action unless it belong to the vegetable kingdom, or the family of sensitive creatures. But the metals are elementary objects, and possess neither seed nor sensation." [1]

His theory of the origin of the metals is astral rather than phallic. "The only efficient cause of metals," he says, " is the mineral virtue, which is not found in every kind of earth, but only in certain places and chosen mines, into which the celestial sphere pours its rays in a straight direction year by year, and according to the arrangement of the metallic substance in these places, this or that metal is gradually formed." [2]

In view of the astrological symbolism of these metals, that gold should be masculine, silver feminine, does not surprise us, because the idea of the masculinity of the sun and the femininity of the moon is a bit of phallicism that still remains with us. It was by the marriage of gold and silver that very many alchemists considered that the *magnum opus* was to be achieved. Writes BERNARD of TRÉVISAN : "The subject of this admired Science [alchemy] is *Sol* and *Luna*, or rather Male and Female, the Male is hot and dry, the Female cold and moyst." The aim of the work, he tells us, is the extraction of the spirit of gold, which alone can enter into bodies and tinge them. Both *Sol* and *Luna* are absolutely necessary, and " whoever . . . shall think that a Tincture can be made without these two Bodyes,

[1] THOMAS NORTON : *The Ordinal of Alchemy.* (See *The Hermetic Museum,* vol. ii. pp. 15 and 16.)
[2] *Ibid.,* pp. 15 and 16.

PLATE 23.

Fig. 44.

Symbolic Alchemical Design illustrating Lactation, from MAIER'S
Atalanta Fugiens.

(*By permission of the British Museum. Photo by Donald Macbeth, London.*)

. . . he proceedeth to the Practice like one that is blind." [1]

KELLY has teaching to the same effect, the Mercury of the Philosophers being for him the menstruum or medium wherein the copulation of Gold with Silver is to be accomplished. Mercury, in fact, seems to have been everything and to have been capable of effecting everything in the eyes of the alchemists. Concerning gold and silver, KELLY writes : " Only one metal, viz. gold, is absolutely perfect and mature. Hence it is called the perfect male body. . . Silver is less bounded by aqueous immaturity than the rest of the metals, though it may indeed be regarded as to a certain extent impure, still its water is already covered with the congealing vesture of its earth, and it thus tends to perfection. This condition is the reason why silver is everywhere called by the Sages the perfect female body." And later he writes : " In short, our whole Magistery consists in the union of the male and female, or active and passive, elements through the mediation of our metallic water and a proper degree of heat. Now, the male and female are two metallic bodies, and this I will again prove by irrefragable quotations from the Sages." Some of the quotations will be given : " Avicenna : ' Purify husband and wife separately, in order that they may unite more intimately ; for if you do not purify them, they cannot love each other. By conjunction of the two natures you get a clear and lucid nature, which, when it ascends, becomes bright and serviceable.' . . . Senior : ' I, the Sun, am hot

[1] BERNARD, Earl of TRÉVISAN : *A Treatise, etc., Op. cit.,* pp. 83 and 87.

and dry, and thou, the Moon, are cold and moist ;
when we are wedded together in a closed chamber, I
will gently steal away thy soul.' . . . Rosinus :
' When the Sun, my brother, for the love of me
(silver) pours his sperm (*i.e.* his solar fatness) into
the chamber (*i.e.* my Lunar body), namely, when we
become one in a strong and complete complexion
and union, the child of our wedded love will be born.'
. . . ' Rosary ' : ' The ferment of the Sun is the
sperm of the man, the ferment of the Moon, the
sperm of the woman.   Of both we get a chaste union
and a true generation.' . . . Aristotle : ' Take your
beloved son, and wed him to his sister, his white
sister, in equal marriage, and give them the cup of
love, for it is a food which prompts to union.' " [1]
KELLY, of course, accepts the traditional authorship
of the works from which he quotes, though in many
cases such authorship is doubtful, to say the least.
The alchemical works ascribed to ARISTOTLE (384–322
B.C.), for instance, are beyond question forgeries.   Indeed, the symbol of a union between brother and
sister, here quoted, could hardly be held as acceptable
to Greek thought, to which incest was the most
abominable and unforgiveable sin.   It seems likelier
that it originated with the Egyptians, to whom such
unions were tolerable in fact.   The symbol is often
met with in Latin alchemy.   MICHAEL MAIER (1568–
1622) also says : " *Conjunge fratrem cum sorore et
propina illis poculum amoris,*" the words forming a
motto to a picture of a man and woman clasped in
each other's arms, to whom an older man offers a

---

[1] EDWARD KELLY : *The Stone of the Philosophers, Op. cit.,*
pp. 13, 14, 33, 35, 36, 38–40, and 47.

FIG. 45.
Symbolic Alchemical Design illustrating the Conjunction of Gold and
Silver (or Sun and Moon), from MAIER's *Atalanta Fugiens.*

goblet. This symbolic picture occurs in his *Atalanta Fugiens, hoc est, Emblemata nova de Secretis Naturæ Chymica, etc.* (Oppenheim, 1617). This work is an exceedingly curious one. It consists of a number of carefully executed pictures, each accompanied by a motto, a verse of poetry set to music, with a prose text. Many of the pictures are phallic in conception, and practically all of them are anthropomorphic. Not only the primary function of sex, but especially its secondary one of lactation, is made use of. The most curious of these emblematic pictures, perhaps, is one symbolising the conjunction of gold and silver. It shows on the right a man and woman, representing the sun and moon, in the act of coition, standing up to the thighs in a lake. On the left, on a hill above the lake, a woman (with the moon as halo) gives birth to a child. A boy is coming out of the water towards her. The verse informs us that : " The bath glows red at the conception of the boy, the air at his birth." We learn also that " there is a stone, and yet there is not, which is the noble gift of God. If God grants it, fortunate will be he who shall receive it." [1]

Concerning the nature of gold, there is a discussion in *The Answer of* BERNARDUS TREVISANUS *to the Epistle of Thomas of Bononia*, with which I shall close my consideration of the present aspect of the subject. Its interest for us lies in the arguments which are used and held to be valid. " Besides, you say that Gold, as most think, is nothing else than *Quick-silver* coagulated naturally by the force of *Sulphur* ; yet so, that nothing of the *Sulphur* which generated the Gold, doth remain in the substance of the Gold : as

[1] *Op. cit.,* p. 145.

in an humane *Embryo*, when it is conceived in the Womb, there remains nothing of the Father's Seed, according to *Aristotle's* opinion, but the Seed of the Man doth only coagulate the *menstrual* blood of the Woman : in the same manner you say, that after *Quick-silver* is so coagulated, the form of Gold is perfected in it, by virtue of the Heavenly Bodies, and especially of the Sun." [1] BERNARD, however, decides against this view, holding that gold contains both mercury and sulphur, for " we must not imagine, according to their mistake who say, that the Male Agent himself approaches the Female in the coagulation, and departs afterwards ; because, as is known in every generation, the conception is active and passive : Both the active and the passive, that is, all the four Elements, must always abide together, otherwise there would be no mixture, and the hope of generating an off-spring would be extinguished." [2]

In conclusion, I wish to say something of the rôle of sex in spiritual alchemy. But in doing this I am venturing outside the original field of inquiry of this essay and making a by no means necessary addition to my thesis ; and I am anxious that what follows should be understood as such, so that no confusion as to the issues may arise.

In the great alchemical collection of J. J. MANGET, there is a curious work (originally published in 1677), entitled *Mutus Liber*, which consists entirely of plates, without letterpress. Its interest for us in our present concern is that the alchemist, from the commencement of the work until its achievement, is

---

[1] *Op. cit.*, pp. 206 and 207.
[2] *Ibid.*, pp. 212 and 213.

FIG. 46.
Symbolic Alchemical Design from *Mutus Liber* (1677).

shown working in conjunction with a woman. We are reminded of NICOLAS FLAMEL (1330–1418), who is reputed to have achieved the *magnum opus* together with his wife PERNELLE, as well as of the many other women workers in the Art of whom we read. It would be of interest in this connection to know exactly what association of ideas was present in the mind of MICHAEL MAIER when he commanded the alchemist : " Perform a work of women on the molten white lead, that is, cook," [1] and illustrated his behest with a picture of a pregnant woman watching a fire over which is suspended a cauldron and on which are three jars. There is a cat in the background, and a tub containing two fish in the foreground, the whole forming a very curious collection of emblems. Mr WAITE, who has dealt with some of these matters, luminously, though briefly, says : " The evidences with which we have been dealing concern solely the physical work of alchemy and there is nothing of its mystical aspects. The *Mutus Liber* is undoubtedly on the literal side of metallic transmutation ; the memorials of Nicholas Flamel are also on that side," *etc*. He adds, however, that " It is on record that an unknown master testified to his possession of the mystery, but he added that he had not proceeded to the work because he had failed to meet with an elect woman who was necessary thereto " ; and proceeds to say : " I suppose that the statement will awaken in most minds only a vague sense of wonder, and I can merely indicate in a few general words that which I see behind it. Those Hermetic texts which bear a spiritual interpretation

[1] MICHAEL MAIER : *Atalanta Fugiens* (1617), p. 97.

and are as if a record of spiritual experience present,
like the literature of physical alchemy, the following
aspects of symbolism : (*a*) the marriage of sun and
moon ; (*b*) of a mystical king and queen ; (*c*) an
union between natures which are one at the root but
diverse in manifestation ; (*d*) a transmutation which
follows this union and an abiding glory therein.   It
is ever a conjunction between male and female in a
mystical sense ; it is ever the bringing together by
art of things separated by an imperfect order of
things ; it is ever the perfection of natures by means
of this conjunction. But if the mystical work of
alchemy is an inward work in consciousness, then
the union between male and female is an union in
consciousness ; and if we remember the traditions
of a state when male and female had not as yet been
divided, it may dawn upon us that the higher alchemy
was a practice for the return into this ineffable mode
of being. The traditional doctrine is set forth in
the *Zohar* and it is found in writers like Jacob
Boehme ; it is intimated in the early chapters of
Genesis and, according to an apocryphal saying of
Christ, the kingdom of heaven will be manifested
when two shall be as one, or when that state has been
once again attained.   In the light of this construction
we can understand why the mystical adept went in
search of a wise woman with whom the work could
be performed ; but few there be that find her, and
he confessed to his own failure. The part of
woman in the physical practice of alchemy is like a
reflection at a distance of this more exalted process,
and there is evidence that those who worked in
metals and sought for a material elixir knew that

FIG. 47.

Symbolic Alchemical Design illustrating the Work of Woman, from MAIER'S *Atalanta Fugiens.*

(*By permission of the British Museum. Photo by Donald Macbeth, London.*)

there were other and greater aspects of the Hermetic mystery." [1]

So far Mr WAITE, whose impressive words I have quoted at some length ; and he has given us a fuller account of the theory as found in the *Zohar* in his valuable work on *The Secret Doctrine in Israel* (1913). The *Zohar* regards marriage and the performance of the sexual function in marriage as of supreme importance, and this not merely because marriage symbolises a divine union, unless that expression is held to include all that logically follows from the fact, but because, as it seems, the sexual act in marriage may, in fact, become a ritual of transcendental magic.

At least three varieties of opinion can be traced from the view of sex we have under consideration, as to the nature of the perfect man, and hence of the most adequate symbol for transmutation. According to one, and this appears to have been JACOB BOEHME's view, the perfect man is conceived of as non-sexual, the male and female elements united in him having, as it were, neutralised each other. According to another, he is pictured as a hermaphroditic being, a concept we frequently come across in alchemical literature. It plays a prominent part in MAIER's book *Atalanta Fugiens*, to which reference has already been made. MAIER's hermaphrodite has two heads, one male, one female, but only one body, one pair of arms, and one pair of legs. The two sexual organs, which are placed side by side, are delineated in the illustrations with considerable care,

[1] A. E. WAITE : " Woman and the Hermetic Mystery," *The Occult Review* (June 1912), vol. xv. pp. 325 and 326.

showing the importance MAIER attached to the idea.
This concept seems to me not only crude, but un-
natural and repellent. But it may be said of both
the opinions I have mentioned, that they confuse
between union and identity. It is the old mistake,
with respect to a lesser goal, of those who hope for
absorption in the Divine Nature and consequent loss
of personality. It seems to be forgotten that a
certain degree of distinction is necessary to the joy
of union. " Distinction " and " separation," it
should be remembered, have different connotations.
If the supreme joy is that of self-sacrifice, then the
self must be such that it can be continually sacrificed,
else the joy is a purely transitory one, or rather, is
destroyed at the moment of its consummation.
Hence, though sacrificed, the self must still remain
itself.

The third view of perfection, to which these remarks naturally lead, is that which sees it typified
in marriage. The mystic-philosopher SWEDEN-
BORG has some exceedingly suggestive things to say
on the matter in his extraordinary work on *Conjugial
Love*, which, curiously enough, seem largely to
have escaped the notice of students of these high
mysteries.

SWEDENBORG'S heaven is a sexual heaven, because
for him sex is primarily a spiritual fact, and only
secondarily, and because of what it is primarily, a
physical fact; and salvation is hardly possible,
according to him, apart from a genuine marriage
(whether achieved here or hereafter). Man and
woman are considered as complementary beings,
and it is only through the union of one man with

FIG. 48.

Symbolic Alchemical Design, Hermaphrodite, from MAIER's *Atalanta Fugiens*.

(*By permission of the British Museum.   Photo by Donald Macbeth, London.*)

one woman that the perfect angel results. The altruistic tendency of such a theory as contrasted with the egotism of one in which perfection is regarded as obtainable by each personality of itself alone, is a point worth emphasising. As to the nature of this union, it is, to use SWEDENBORG'S own terms, a conjunction of the will of the wife with the understanding of the man, and reciprocally of the understanding of the man with the will of the wife. It is thus a manifestation of that fundamental marriage between the good and the true which is at the root of all existence; and it is because of this fundamental marriage that all men and women are born into the desire to complete themselves by conjunction. The symbol of sexual intercourse is a legitimate one to use in speaking of this heavenly union; indeed, we may describe the highest bliss attainable by the soul, or conceivable by the mind, as a spiritual orgasm. Into conjugial love "are collected," says SWEDENBORG, " all the blessednesses, blissfulnesses, delightsomenesses, pleasantnesses, and pleasures, which could possibly be conferred upon man by the Lord the Creator." [1] In another place he writes: " Married partners [in heaven] enjoy similar intercourse with each other as in the world, but more delightful and blessed; yet without prolification, for which, or in place of which, they have spiritual prolification, which is that of love and wisdom." "The reason," he adds, "why the intercourse then is more delightful and blessed is, that when conjugial love becomes of the spirit, it becomes

[1] EMANUEL SWEDENBORG : *The Delights of Wisdom relating to Conjugial Love* (trans. by A. H. SEARLE, 1891), § 68.

more interior and pure, and consequently more perceptible; and every delightsomeness grows according to the perception, and grows even until its blessedness is discernible in its delightsomeness." [1] Such love, however, he says, is rarely to be found on earth.

A learned Japanese speaks with approval of Idealism as a " dream where sensuousness and spirituality find themselves to be blood brothers or sisters." [2] It is a statement which involves either the grossest and most dangerous error, or the profoundest truth, according to the understanding of it. Woman is a road whereby man travels either to God or the devil. The problem of sex is a far deeper problem than appears at first sight, involving mysteries both the direst and most holy. It is by no means a fantastic hypothesis that the inmost mystery of what a certain school of mystics calls " the Secret Tradition " was a sexual one. At any rate, the fact that some of those, at least, to whom alchemy connoted a mystical process, were alive to the profound spiritual significance of sex, renders of double interest what they have to intimate of the achievement of the *Magnum Opus* in man.

[1] EMANUEL SWEDENBORG : *Op. cit.*, § 51.
[2] YONE NOGUCHI : *The Spirit of Japanese Art* (1915), p. 37.

XI

ROGER BACON : AN
APPRECIATION

IT has been said that " a prophet is not without
honour, save in his own country." Thereto might
be added, " and in his own time " ; for, whilst
there is continuity in time, there is also evolution,
and England of to-day, for instance, is not the same
country as England of the Middle Ages. In his
own day ROGER BACON was accounted a magician,
whose heretical views called for suppression by the
Church. And for many a long day afterwards was
he mainly remembered as a co-worker in the black
art with Friar BUNGAY, who together with him constructed, by the aid of the devil and diabolical rites,
a brazen head which should possess the power of
speech—the experiment only failing through the
negligence of an assistant.[1] Such was ROGER BACON
in the memory of the later Middle Ages and many
succeeding years ; he was the typical alchemist,

[1] The story, of course, is entirely fictitious. For further
particulars see Sir J. E. SANDYS' essay on " Roger Bacon in
English Literature," in *Roger Bacon Essays* (1914), referred to
below.

where that term carries with it the depth of disrepute, though indeed alchemy was for him but one, and that not the greatest, of many interests.

Ilchester, in Somerset, claims the honour of being the place of ROGER BACON'S birth, which interesting and important event occurred, probably, in 1214. Young BACON studied theology, philosophy, and what then passed under the name of " science," first at Oxford, then the centre of liberal thought, and afterwards at Paris, in the rigid orthodoxy of whose professors he found more to criticise than to admire. Whilst at Oxford he joined the Franciscan Order, and at Paris he is said, though this is probably an error, to have graduated as Doctor of Theology. During 1250–1256 we find him back in England, no doubt engaged in study and teaching. About the latter year, however, he is said to have been banished—on a charge of holding heterodox views and indulging in magical practices—to Paris, where he was kept in close confinement and forbidden to write. Mr LITTLE,[1] however, believes this to be an error, based on a misreading of a passage in one of BACON'S works, and that ROGER was not imprisoned, but stricken with sickness. At any rate it is not improbable that some restrictions as to his writing were placed on him by his superiors of the Franciscan Order. In 1266 BACON received a letter from Pope CLEMENT asking him to send His Holiness his works in writing without delay. This letter came as a most pleasant surprise to BACON ; but he had nothing of importance written, and in great haste and excite-

[1] See his contribution, " On Roger Bacon's Life and Works," to *Roger Bacon Essays*.

Fig. 49.

ROGER BACON presenting a Book to a King, from a Fifteenth-century
Miniature in the Bodleian Library, Oxford.

[NOTE.—There is no contemporary portrait of Roger Bacon known, so that the authenticity
of every one of the portraits alleged to be of him is open to doubt. The two reproduced in
figs. 49 and 50 are probably the oldest extant, and are therefore the most worthy of respect.
That from the Bodleian Library is reproduced by kind permission of the authorities, and is, I
think, the earliest known portrait of Bacon. The Knole Castle portrait (fig. 50) is by an unknown artist, probably of the Elizabethan period. It is reproduced by permission of Lady
Sackville.]

ment, therefore, he composed three works explicating his philosophy, the *Opus Majus*, the *Opus Minus*, and the *Opus Tertium*, which were completed and dispatched to the Pope by the end of the following year. This, as Mr ROWBOTTOM remarks, is " surely one of the literary feats of history, perhaps only surpassed by Swedenborg when he wrote six theological and philosophical treatises in one year." [1]

The works appear to have been well received. We next find BACON at Oxford writing his *Compendium Studii Philosophiæ*, in which work he indulged in some by no means unjust criticisms of the clergy, for which he fell under the condemnation of his order, and was imprisoned in 1277 on a charge of teaching " suspected novelties ". In those days any knowledge of natural phenomena beyond that of the quasi-science of the times was regarded as magic, and no doubt some of ROGER BACON'S " suspected novelties " were of this nature ; his recognition of the value of the writings of non-Christian moralists was, no doubt, another "suspected novelty". Appeals for his release directed to the Pope proved fruitless, being frustrated by JEROME D'ASCOLI, General of the Franciscan Order, who shortly afterwards succeeded to the Holy See under the title of NICHOLAS IV. The latter died in 1292, whereupon RAYMUND GAUFREDI, who had been elected General of the Franciscan Order, and who, it is thought, was well disposed towards BACON, because of certain alchemical secrets the latter had revealed to him, ordered his release. BACON returned to Oxford, where he wrote

[1] B. R. ROWBOTTOM: " Roger Bacon," *The Journal of the Alchemical Society*, vol. ii. (1914), p. 77.

his last work, the *Compendium Studii Theologiæ*.
He died either in this year or in 1294.[1]

It was not until the publication by Dr SAMUEL
JEBB, in 1733, of the greater part of BACON's *Opus
Majus*, nearly four and a half centuries after his
death, that anything like his rightful position in the
history of philosophy began to be assigned to him.
But let his spirit be no longer troubled, if it were
ever troubled by neglect or slander, for the world,
and first and foremost his own country, has paid
him due honour. His septcentenary was duly celebrated in 1914 at his *alma mater*, Oxford, his statue
has there been raised as a memorial to his greatness,
and savants have meted out praise to him in no
grudging tones.[2] Indeed, a voice has here and there
been heard depreciating his better-known namesake
FRANCIS,[3] so that the later luminary should not,
standing in the way, obscure the light of the earlier;
though, for my part, I would suggest that one need
not be so one-eyed as to fail to see both lights at once.

To those who like to observe coincidences, it may

[1] For further details concerning BACON's life, EMILE
CHARLES: *Roger Bacon, sa Vie, ses Ouvrages, ses Doctrines*
(1861); J. H. BRIDGES: *The Life & Work of Roger Bacon, an
Introduction to the Opus Majus* (edited by H. G. JONES, 1914);
and Mr A. G. LITTLE's essay in *Roger Bacon Essays*, may be
consulted.

[2] See *Roger Bacon, Essays contributed by various Writers on
the Occasion of the Commemoration of the Seventh Centenary of
his Birth.* Collected and edited by A. G. LITTLE (1914); also
Sir J. E. SANDYS' *Roger Bacon* (from *The Proceedings of the
British Association*, vol. vi., 1914).

[3] For example, that of ERNST DUHRING. See an article
entitled "The Two Bacons," translated from his *Kritische
Geschichte der Philosophie* in *The Open Court* for August 1914.

be of interest that the septcentenary of the discoverer of gunpowder should have coincided with the outbreak of the greatest war under which the world has yet groaned, even though gunpowder is no longer employed as a military propellant.

Bacon's reference to gunpowder occurs in his *Epistola de Secretis Operibus Artis et Naturæ, et de Nullitate Magiæ* (Hamburg, 1618) a little tract written against magic, in which he endeavours to show, and succeeds very well in the first eight chapters, that Nature and art can perform far more extraordinary feats than are claimed by the workers in the black art. The last three chapters are written in an alchemical jargon of which even one versed in the symbolic language of alchemy can make no sense. They are evidently cryptogramic, and probably deal with the preparation and purification of saltpetre, which had only recently been discovered as a distinct body.[1] In chapter xi. there is reference to an explosive body, which can only be gunpowder; by means of it, says Bacon, you may, " if you know the trick, produce a bright flash and a thundering noise." He mentions two of the ingredients, saltpetre and sulphur, but conceals the third (*i.e.* charcoal) under an anagram. Claims have, indeed, been put forth for the Greek, Arab, Hindu, and Chinese origins of gunpowder, but a close examination of the original ancient accounts purporting to contain references to gunpowder,

---

[1] For an attempted explanation of this cryptogram, and evidence that Bacon was the discoverer of gunpowder, see Lieut.-Col. H. W. L. Hime's *Gunpowder and Ammunition: their Origin and Progress* (1904).

shows that only incendiary and not explosive bodies are really dealt with. But whilst ROGER BACON knew of the explosive property of a mixture in right proportions of sulphur, charcoal, and pure saltpetre (which he no doubt accidentally hit upon whilst experimenting with the last-named body), he was unaware of its projective power. That discovery, so detrimental to the happiness of man ever since, was, in all probability, due to BERTHOLD SCHWARZ about 1330.

ROGER BACON has been credited [1] with many other discoveries. In the work already referred to he allows his imagination freely to speculate as to the wonders that might be accomplished by a scientific utilisation of Nature's forces—marvellous things with lenses, in bringing distant objects near and so forth, carriages propelled by mechanical means, flying machines . . .—but in no case is the word "discovery" in any sense applicable, for not even in the case of the telescope does BACON describe means by which his speculations might be realised.

On the other hand, ROGER BACON has often been maligned for his beliefs in astrology and alchemy, but, as the late Dr BRIDGES (who was quite sceptical of the claims of both) pointed out, not to have believed in them in BACON's day would have been rather an evidence of mental weakness than otherwise. What relevant facts were known supported alchemical and astrological hypotheses. Astrology, Dr BRIDGES writes, "conformed to the first law of Comte's

[1] For instance by Mr M. M. P. MUIR. See his contribution, on "Roger Bacon : His Relations to Alchemy and Chemistry," to *Roger Bacon Essays.*

PLATE 29.

FIG. 50.

ROGER BACON, from a Portrait in Knole Castle.

(Copyright by C. Essenheigh-Corke, Sevenoaks. See Note on Plate 28.)

philosophia prima, as being the best hypothesis of which ascertained phenomena admitted." [1] And in his alchemical speculations BACON was much in advance of his contemporaries, and stated problems which are amongst those of modern chemistry.

ROGER BACON'S greatness does not lie in the fact that he discovered gunpowder, nor in the further fact that his speculations have been validated by other men. His greatness lies in his secure grip of scientific method as a combination of mathematical reasoning and experiment. Men before him had experimented, but none seemed to have realised the importance of the experimental method. Nor was he, of course, by any means the first mathematician—there was a long line of Greek and Arabian mathematicians behind him, men whose knowledge of the science was in many cases much greater than his— or the most learned mathematician of his day ; but none realised the importance of mathematics as an organon of scientific research as he did ; and he was assuredly the priest who joined mathematics to experiment in the bonds of sacred matrimony. We must not, indeed, look for precise rules of inductive reasoning in the works of this pioneer writer on scientific method. Nor do we find really satisfactory rules of induction even in the works of FRANCIS BACON. Moreover, the latter despised mathematics, and it was not until in quite recent years that the scientific world came to realise that ROGER'S method is the more fruitful—witness the modern revolution in chemistry produced by the adoption of mathematical methods.

[1] *Op. cit.*, p. 84.

ROGER BACON, it may be said, was many centuries in advance of his time ; but it is equally true that he was the child of his time ; this may account for his defects judged by modern standards. He owed not a little to his contemporaries : for his knowledge and high estimate of philosophy he was largely indebted to his Oxford master GROSSETESTE (*c.* 1175–1253), whilst PETER PEREGRINUS, his friend at Paris, fostered his love of experiment, and the Arab mathematicians, whose works he knew, inclined his mind to mathematical studies. He was violently opposed to the scholastic views current in Paris at his time, and attacked great thinkers like THOMAS AQUINAS (*c.* 1225–1274) and ALBERTUS MAGNUS (1193–1280), as well as obscurantists, such as ALEXANDER of HALES (*ob.* 1245). But he himself was a scholastic philosopher, though of no servile type, taking part in scholastic arguments. If he declared that he would have all the works of ARISTOTLE burned, it was not because he hated the Peripatetic's philosophy—though he could criticise as well as appreciate at times,—but because of the rottenness of the translations that were then used. It seems commonplace now, but it was a truly wonderful thing then : ROGER BACON believed in accuracy, and was by no means destitute of literary ethics. He believed in correct translation, correct quotation, and the acknowledgment of the sources of one's quotations—unheard-of things, almost, in those days. But even he was not free from all the vices of his age : in spite of his insistence upon experimental verification of the conclusions of deductive reasoning, in one place, at least, he adopts a view concerning lenses from another writer, of which the simplest attempt at such verification would have revealed the falsity. For such lapses, however, we can make allowances.

Another and undeniable claim to greatness rests on ROGER BACON's broad-mindedness. He could actually value at their true worth the moral philosophies of non-Christian writers—SENECA (*c.* 5 B.C.–A.D. 65) and AL GHAZZALI (1058–1111), for instance. But if he was catholic in the original meaning of that term, he was also catholic in its restricted sense. He was no heretic : the Pope for him was the Vicar of CHRIST, whom he wished to see reign over the whole world, not by force of arms, but by the assimilation of all that was worthy in that world. To his mind—and here he was certainly a child of his age, in its best sense, perhaps—all other sciences were handmaidens to theology, queen of them all. All were to be subservient to her aims : the Church he called " Catholic " was to embrace in her arms all that was worthy in the works of " profane " writers—true prophets of God, he held, in so far as writing worthily they unconsciously bore testimony to the truth of Christianity,—and all that Nature might yield by patient experiment and speculation guided by mathematics. Some minds see in this a defect in his system, which limited his aims and outlook ; others see it as the unifying principle giving coherence to the whole. At any rate, the Church, as we have seen, regarded his views as dangerous, and restrained his pen for at least a considerable portion of his life.

ROGER BACON may seem egotistic in argument, but his mind was humble to learn. He was not superstitious, but he would listen to common folk who worked with their hands, to astrologers, and even magicians, denying nothing which seemed to him to have some evidence in experience : if he denied much of magical belief, it was because he found it lacking in such evidence. He often went astray in his views; he sometimes failed to apply his own method, and that method was, in any case, primitive and crude. But it was the *right* method, in embryo at least, and ROGER BACON, in spite of tremendous opposition, greater than that under which any man of science may now suffer, persisted in that method to the end, calling upon his contemporaries to adopt it as the only one which results in right knowledge. Across the centuries—or, rather, across the gulf that divides this world from the next—let us salute this great and noble spirit.

XII

THE CAMBRIDGE PLATONISTS

THERE is an opinion, unfortunately very common, that religious mysticism is a product of the emotional temperament, and is diametrically opposed to the spirit of rationalism. No doubt this opinion is not without some element of justification, and one could quote the works of not a few religious mystics to the effect that self-surrender to God implies, not merely a giving up of will, but also of reason. But that this teaching is not an essential element in mysticism, that it is, indeed, rather its perversion, there is adequate evidence to demonstrate. SWEDENBORG is, I suppose, the outstanding instance of an intellectual mystic ; but the essential unity of mysticism and rationalism is almost as forcibly made evident in the case of the Cambridge Platonists. That little band of " Latitude men," as their contemporaries called them, constitutes one of the finest schools of philosophy that England has produced ; yet their works are rarely read, I am afraid, save by specialists. Possibly, however, if it were more commonly known what a wealth of sound philosophy and true spiritual teaching they contain, the case would be otherwise.

The Cambridge Platonists—BENJAMIN WHICHCOTE, JOHN SMITH, NATHANAEL CULVERWEL, RALPH CUDWORTH, and HENRY MORE are the more outstanding names—were educated as Puritans; but they clearly realised the fundamental error of Puritanism, which tended to make a man's eternal salvation depend upon the accuracy and extent of his beliefs; nor could they approve of the exaggerated import given by the High Church party to matters of Church polity. The term "Cambridge Platonists" is, perhaps, less appropriate than that of "Latitudinarians," which latter name emphasises their broad-mindedness (even if it carries with it something of disapproval). For although they owed much to PLATO, and, perhaps, more to PLOTINUS (c. A.D. 203–262), they were Christians first and Platonists afterwards, and, with the exception, perhaps, of MORE, they took nothing from these philosophers which was not conformable to the Scriptures.

BENJAMIN WHICHCOTE was born in 1609, at Whichcote Hall, in the parish of Stoke, Shropshire. In 1626 he entered Emmanuel College, Cambridge, then regarded as the chief Puritan college of the University. Here his college tutor was ANTHONY TUCKNEY (1599–1670), a man of rare character, combining learning, wit, and piety. Between WHICHCOTE and TUCKNEY there grew up a firm friendship, founded on mutual affection and esteem. But TUCKNEY was unable to agree with all WHICHCOTE's broad-minded views concerning reason and authority;

Beniamin Whichcot *S. S. T. Professor*

FIG. 51.

BENJAMIN WHICHCOTE, from an engraved Portrait by ROBERT WHITE.

and in later years this gave rise to a controversy between them, in which TUCKNEY sought to controvert WHICHCOTE's opinions : it was, however, carried on without acrimony, and did not destroy their friendship.

WHICHCOTE became M.A., and was elected a fellow of his college, in 1633, having obtained his B.A. four years previously. He was ordained by JOHN WILLIAMS in 1636, and received the important appointment of Sunday afternoon lecturer at Trinity Church. His lectures, which he gave with the object of turning men's minds from polemics to the great moral and spiritual realities at the basis of the Christian religion, from mere formal discussions to a true searching into the reason of things, were well attended and highly appreciated ; and he held the appointment for twenty years. In 1634 he became college tutor at Emmanuel. He possessed all the characteristics that go to make up an efficient and well-beloved tutor, and his personal influence was such as to inspire all his pupils, amongst whom were both JOHN SMITH and NATHANAEL CULVERWEL, who considerably amplified his philosophical and religious doctrines. In 1640 he became B.D., and nine years after was created D.D. The college living of North Cadbury, in Somerset, was presented to him in 1643, and shortly afterwards he married. In the next year, however, he was recalled to Cambridge, and installed as Provost of King's College in place of the ejected Dr SAMUEL COLLINS. But it was greatly against his wish that he received the appointment, and he only consented to do so on the condition that part of his stipend should be paid to COLLINS—an act which gives us a good insight into the character of the man. In 1650 he resigned North Cadbury, and the living was presented to CUDWORTH (see below), and towards the end of this year he was elected Vice-Chancellor of the University in succession to TUCKNEY. It was during his Vice-Chancellorship that he preached the sermon that gave rise to the controversy with the latter. About this time also he was presented with the living of Milton, in Cambridgeshire. At the Restoration he was ejected from the Provostship, but, having complied with the Act of Uniformity, he was, in 1662, appointed to the cure of St Anne's, Blackfriars. This church being destroyed in the Great Fire, WHICHCOTE retired to Milton, where he showed great kindness to the poor. But some years later he returned to London, having received the vicarage of St Lawrence, Jewry. His friends at Cambridge, however, still saw him on occasional visits, and it was on one such visit to CUDWORTH, in 1683, that he caught the cold which caused his death.

JOHN SMITH was born at Achurch, near Oundle, in 1618. He entered Emmanuel College in 1636, became B.A. in 1640, and proceeded to M.A. in 1644, in which year he was appointed a fellow of Queen's College. Here he lectured on arithmetic with considerable success. He was noted for his great learning, especially in theology and Oriental languages, as well as for his justness, uprightness, and humility. He died of consumption in 1652.

NATHANAEL CULVERWEL was probably born about the same year as SMITH. He entered Emmanuel College in 1633, gained his B.A. in 1636, and became M.A. in 1640. Soon afterwards he was elected a fellow of his college. He died about 1651. Beyond these scant details, nothing is known of his life. He was a man of very great erudition, as his posthumous treatise on *The Light of Nature* makes evident.

HENRY MORE was born at Grantham in 1614. From his earliest days he was interested in theological problems, and his precociousness in this respect appears to have brought down on him the wrath of an uncle. His early education was conducted at Eton. In 1631 he entered Christ's College, Cambridge, graduated B.A. in 1635, and received his M.A. in 1639. In the latter year he was elected a fellow of Christ's and received Holy Orders. He lived a very retired life, refusing all preferment, though many valuable and honourable appointments were offered to him. Indeed, he rarely left Christ's, except to visit his " heroine pupil," Lady CONWAY, whose country seat, Ragley, was in Warwickshire. Lady CONWAY (*ob.* 1679) appears to be remembered only for the fact that, dying whilst her husband was away, her physician, F. M. VAN HELMONT (1618–1699) (son of the famous alchemist, J. B. VAN HELMONT, whom we have met already on these excursions), preserved her body in spirits of wine, so that he could have the pleasure of beholding it on his return. She seems to have been a woman of considerable learning, though not free from fantastic ideas. Her ultimate conversion to Quakerism was a severe blow to MORE, who, whilst admiring the holy lives of the Friends, regarded them as enthusiasts. MORE died in 1687.

MORE's earliest works were in verse, and exhibit fine feeling. The following lines, quoted from a poem on " Charitie and Humilitie," are full of charm, and well exhibit MORE's character :—

> " Farre have I clambred in my mind
>   But nought so great as love I find :
>   Deep-searching wit, mount-moving might,
>   Are nought compar'd to that great spright.
>   Life of Delight and soul of blisse !
>   Sure source of lasting happinesse !
>   Higher than Heaven ! lower than hell !
>   What is thy tent ?   Where maist thou dwell ?
>   My mansion hight humilitie,
>   Heaven's vastest capabilitie
>   The further it doth downward tend
>   The higher up it doth ascend ;
>   If it go down to utmost nought
>   It shall return with that it sought." [1]

Later he took to prose, and it must be confessed that he wrote too much and frequently descended to polemics (for example, his controversy with the alchemist THOMAS VAUGHAN, in which both combatants freely used abuse).

Although in his main views MORE is thoroughly characteristic of the school to which he belonged, many of his less important opinions are more or less peculiar to himself.

The relation between MORE's and DESCARTES' (1596–1650) theories as to the nature of spirit is interesting. When MORE first read DESCARTES'

---

[1] See The Life of the Learned and Pious Dr Henry More . . . by RICHARD WARD, A.M., to which are annexed Divers Philosophical Poems and Hymns. Edited by M. F. HOWARD (1911), pp. 250 and 251.

FIG. 52.

HENRY MORE, from a Portrait by DAVID LOGGAN, engraved *ad vivum*, 1679.

works he was favourably impressed with his views, though without entirely agreeing with him on all points ; but later the difference became accentuated. DESCARTES regarded extension as the chief characteristic of matter, and asserted that spirit was extra-spatial. To MORE this seemed like denying the existence of spirit, which he regarded as extended, and he postulated divisibility and impenetrability as the chief characteristics of matter. In order, however, to get over some of the inherent difficulties of this view, he put forward the suggestion that spirit is extended in four dimensions : thus, its apparent (*i.e.* three-dimensional) extension can change, whilst its true (*i.e.* four-dimensional) extension remains constant ; just as the surface of a piece of metal can be increased by hammering it out, without increasing the volume of the metal. Here, I think, we have a not wholly inadequate symbol of the truth ; but it remained for BERKELEY (1685–1753) to show the essential validity of DESCARTES' position, by demonstrating that, since space and extension are perceptions of the mind, and thus exist only in the mind as ideas, space exists in spirit : not spirit in space.

MORE was a keen believer in witchcraft, and eagerly investigated all cases of these and like marvels that came under his notice. In this he was largely influenced by JOSEPH GLANVIL (1636–1680), whose book on witchcraft, the well-known *Saducismus Triumphatus*, MORE largely contributed to, and probably edited. MORE was wholly unsuited for psychical research ; free from guile himself, he was too inclined to judge others to be of this nature also.

But his common sense and critical attitude towards enthusiasm saved him, no doubt, from many falls into the mire of fantasy.

As Principal TULLOCH has pointed out, whilst MORE is the most interesting personality amongst the Cambridge Platonists, his works are the least interesting of those of his school. They are dull and scholastic, and MORE'S retired existence prevented him from grasping in their fulness some of the more acute problems of life. His attempt to harmonise catastrophes with Providence, on the ground that the evil of certain parts may be necessary for the good of the whole, just as dark colours, as well as bright, are essential to the beauty of a picture—a theory which is practically the same as that of modern Absolutism,[1]—is a case in point. No doubt this harmony may be accomplished, but in another key.

RALPH CUDWORTH was born at Aller, in Somersetshire, in 1617. He entered Emmanuel College in 1632, three years afterwards gained his B.A., and became M.A. in 1639. In the latter year he was elected a fellow of his college. Later he obtained the B.D. degree. In 1645 he was appointed Master of Clare Hall, in place of the ejected Dr PASHE, and was elected Regius Professor of Hebrew. On 31st March 1647 he preached a sermon of remarkable eloquence and power before the House of Commons, which admirably expresses the attitude of his school as concerns the nature of true religion. I shall refer to it again later. In 1650 CUDWORTH was presented

[1] Cf. BERNARD BOSANQUET, LL.D., D.C.L.: The Principle of Individuality and Value (1912).

with the college living of North Cadbury, which WHICHCOTE had resigned, and was made D.D. in the following year. In 1654 he was elected Master of Christ's College, with an improvement in his financial position, there having been some difficulty in obtaining his stipend at Clare Hall. In this year he married. In 1662 Bishop SHELDON presented him with the rectory of Ashwell, in Hertfordshire. He died in 1688. He was a pious man of fine intellect ; but his character was marred by a certain suspiciousness which caused him wrongfully to accuse MORE, in 1665, of attempting to forestall him in writing a work on ethics, which should demonstrate that the principles of Christian morality are not based on any arbitrary decrees of God, but are inherent in the nature and reason of things. CUDWORTH'S great work—or, at least, the first part, which alone was completed,—*The Intellectual System of the World*, appeared in 1678. In it CUDWORTH deals with atheism on the ground of reason, demonstrating its irrationality. The book is remarkable for the fairness and fulness with which CUDWORTH states the arguments in favour of atheism.

So much for the lives and individual characteristics of the Cambridge Platonists : what were the great principles that animated both their lives and their philosophy ? These, I think, were two : first, the essential unity of religion and morality ; second, the essential unity of revelation and reason.

With clearer perception of ethical truth than either Puritan or High Churchman, the Cambridge Platonists saw that true Christianity is neither a matter of mere belief, nor consists in the mere performance of good works ; but is rather a matter of character. To them Christianity connoted regeneration. " Religion," says WHICHCOTE, " is the Frame and *Temper* of our Minds, and the *Rule* of our Lives " ; and again, " Heaven is *first* a Temper, and *then* a Place." [1] To the man of heavenly temper, they taught, the performance of good works would be no irksome matter imposed merely by a sense of duty, but would be done spontaneously as a delight. To drudge in religion may very well be necessary as an initial stage, but it is not its perfection.

In his sermon before the House of Commons, CUDWORTH well exposes the error of those who made the mere holding of certain beliefs the essential element in Christianity. There are many passages I should like to quote from this eloquent discourse, but the following must suffice : " We must not judge of our knowing of Christ, by our skill in Books and Papers, but by our keeping of his Commandments. . . . He is the best Christian, whose heart beats with the truest pulse towards heaven ; not he whose head spinneth out the finest cobwebs. He that endeavours really to mortifie his lusts, and to comply with that truth in his life, which his Conscience is convinced of ; is neerer a Christian, though he never heard of Christ ; then he that believes all the vulgar Articles of the Christian faith, and plainly denyeth Christ in his life. . . . The great Mysterie of the Gospel, it doth not lie only in *Christ without us*, (though we must know also what he hath done for us) but the

---

[1] My quotations from WHICHCOTE and SMITH are taken from the selection of their discourses edited by E. T. CAMPAGNAC, M.A. (1901).

very Pith and Kernel of it, consists in *Christ inwardly formed* in our hearts. Nothing is truly Ours, but what lives in our Spirits. *Salvation* it self cannot *save* us, as long as it is onely without us ; no more then *Health* can cure us, and make us sound, when it is not within us, but somewhere at distance from us ; no more than *Arts and Sciences*, whilst they lie onely in Books and Papers without us ; can make us learned." [1]

The Cambridge Platonists were not ascetics ; their moral doctrine was one of temperance. Their sound wisdom on this point is well evident in the following passage from WHICHCOTE : " What can be alledged for Intemperance ; since Nature is content with very few things ? Why should any one over-do in this kind ? A Man is better in Health and Strength, if he be temperate. We enjoy ourselves more in a sober and temperate Use of ourselves." [2]

The other great principle animating their philosophy was, as I have said, the essential unity of reason and revelation. To those who argued that self-surrender implied a giving up of reason, they replied that " To go against *Reason*, is to go against *God* : it is the self same thing, to do that which the Reason of the Case doth require ; and that which God Himself doth appoint : Reason is the *Divine* Governor of Man's Life ; it is the very Voice of God." [3] Reason,

[1] RALPH CUDWORTH, B.D.: *A Sermon Preached before the Honourable House of Commons at Westminster, Mar.* 31, 1647 (1st edn.), pp. 3, 14, 42, and 43.

[2] BENJAMIN WHICHCOTE : *The Venerable Nature and Transcendant Benefit of Christian Religion. Op. cit.*, p. 40.

[3] BENJAMIN WHICHCOTE : *Moral and Religious Aphorisms. Op. cit.*, p. 67.

Conscience, and the Scriptures, these, taught the Cambridge Platonists, testify of one another and are the true guides which alone a man should follow. All other authority they repudiated. But true reason is not merely sensuous, and the only way whereby it may be gained is by the purification of the self from the desires that draw it away from the Source of all Reason. " God," writes MORE, " reserves His choicest secrets for the purest Minds," adding his conviction that " true Holiness [is] the only safe Entrance into Divine Knowledge." Or as SMITH, who speaks of " a *Good life* as the *Prolepsis* and Fundamental principle of *Divine Science*," puts it, " . . . if . . . *Knowledge* be not attended with *Humility* and a deep sense of *Self-penury* and *Self-emptiness*, we may easily fall short of that True Knowledge of God which we seem to aspire after." [1] Right Reason, however, they taught, is the product of the sight of the soul, the true mystic vision.

In what respects, it may be asked in conclusion, is the philosophy of the Cambridge Platonists open to criticism ? They lacked, perhaps, a sufficiently clear concept of the Church as a unity, and although they clearly realised that Nature is a symbol which it is the function of reason to interpret spiritually, they failed, I think, to appreciate the value of symbols. Thus they have little to teach with respect to the Sacraments of the Church, though, indeed, the highest view, perhaps, is that which regards every act

---

[1] JOHN SMITH : *A Discourse concerning the true Way or Method of attaining to Divine Knowledge. Op. cit.*, pp. 80 and 96.

as potentially a sacrament; and, whilst admiring his morality, they criticised BOEHME as an enthusiast. But, although he spoke in a very different language, spiritually he had much in common with them. Compared with what is of positive value in their philosophy, however, the defects of the Cambridge Platonists are but comparatively slight. I commend their works to lovers of spiritual wisdom.

THE END

OTHER SUN BOOKS TITLES
which you may find of interest:

BEST ENGRAVINGS Edited by Skip Whitson
Contains 123 beautiful steel and wood-cut engravings from the Nineteenth Century including: The Spanish Flower Girl, Cherry Earrings, Attack and Defence, Homeless, Dante, The City Belle, The Country Blossom, Priestly Admonition, The Broken Thread, The Professor's Lecture, A Reverie, Mandala, The Resting-Place of the Deer, The Bouquet, Shakspeare, The Children's Offering, The Little Musician, The Syren, Bohemian Wayfarers, Aldarium of the Baths of Caracalla, A Tranquil Hour, Alms Giving, The Confessional, Solitude, Victoria Falls, Hand-Carved Furniture, A Daughter of the East, Aurora, W.H. Seward, MacBeth, The Critic, Dante and the Eagle, The Peacock Complaining to Juno, Aladdin's Gate, Prayer in the Forest, Galatea, Gamesters, A Feast of Cherries, The Hindoo Maiden, A Halt in the Yosemite Valley, The Brothers, The Shepherd, Between School Hours, A Visit From the Inquisitors, Echo Lake, The Eagle's Nest, On the Hill Side, Simpletons, The Seraglio, Maha Toolut-Boungyo, Philogophy and Christian Art, The Dockyard, The Duel Interrupted, Queen of the Vineyard, Sunset, The Dispatch From Trebizond, Detected, Weary!, Pastime in Ancient Egypt, A Tempest in a Teapot, etc.

THE SUN HISTORICAL SERIES Edited by Skip Whitson
This series of 33 titles contains many fine articles and wood-cut illustrations on various cities, regions, and states from Maine to Hawaii. Each book is 8½" x 11", perfect-bound paperback, either 40 or 48 pages. Titles may be purchased individually or as a set. They make a wonderful addition to any library or bookstore.

THE ILLUMINOIDS Secret Societies and Political Paranoia by Neal Wilgus
Altho THE ILLUMINOIDS presents a detailed picture of Adam Weishaupt's revolutionary Order of the Illuminati which was founded on May 1, 1776, the real purpose of this book is to trace the influence of secret societies thruout history — from their legendary roots in earliest times down to modern-day conspiracies behind the sensational headlines. "Neal Wilgus really does think for himself...He has no axe to grind. He is looking for the truth and he is neither gullible nor too cynical to follow up on wild possibilities...The best single reference on the Illuminati in fact and legendry is THE ILLUMINOIDS by Neal Wilgus." --Robert Anton Wilson from his book Cosmic Trigger.

For a **FREE LIST** of other Sun Books titles write: **Book List,** SUN PUBLISHING CO., P.O. Box 4383, Albuquerque, N.M. 87196